# The Mummy's Tomb

## A Play

Ken Hill

Songs by
Alan Klein and Ken Hill

*Samuel French – London*
*New York – Sydney – Toronto – Hollywood*

Copyright © 1981 by Ken Hill and Alan Klein
All Rights Reserved

THE MUMMY'S TOMB is fully protected under the copyright laws of the British Commonwealth, including Canada, the United States of America, and all other countries of the Copyright Union. All rights, including professional and amateur stage productions, recitation, lecturing, public reading, motion picture, radio broadcasting, television and the rights of translation into foreign languages are strictly reserved.

ISBN 978-0-573-11288-1

www.samuelfrench.co.uk
www.samuelfrench.com

---

### For Amateur Production Enquiries

**United Kingdom and World excluding North America**

plays@samuelfrench.co.uk

020 7255 4302/01

Each title is subject to availability from Samuel French, depending upon country of performance.

---

CAUTION: Professional and amateur producers are hereby warned that THE MUMMY'S TOMB is subject to a licensing fee. Publication of this play does not imply availability for performance. Both amateurs and professionals considering a production are strongly advised to apply to the appropriate agent before starting rehearsals, advertising, or booking a theatre. A licensing fee must be paid whether the title is presented for charity or gain and whether or not admission is charged.

The professional rights in this play are controlled by Berlin Associates, 7 Tyers Gate, London SE1 3HX.

No one shall make any changes in this title for the purpose of production. No part of this book may be reproduced, stored in a retrieval system, or transmitted in any form, by any means, now known or yet to be invented, including mechanical, electronic, photocopying, recording, videotaping, or otherwise, without the prior written permission of the publisher. No one shall upload this title, or part of this title, to any social media websites.

The right of Ken Hill and Alan Klein to be identified as author of this work has been asserted in accordance with Section 77 of the Copyright, Designs and Patents Act 1988.

# THE MUMMY'S TOMB

Originally commissioned and produced by the Phoenix Theatre, Leicester, under the direction of Ian Giles, the play was fully revised into its present form and produced at the Theatre Royal, Stratford East on the 8th September 1980, with the following cast of characters—

| | |
|---|---|
| Paul Conway | Francis Thomson |
| Inmutef-Amun | Michael G. Jones |
| Selena | Adrienne Posta |
| Ashayet | Anna Sharkey |
| Pharaoh Amenhotep IV | Richard Tate |
| Mahu | Maynard Williams |
| First Palace Guard | Tony Scannell |
| Second Palace Guard | Bob Packham |
| Professor Niven | Michael Poole |
| Nancy | Adrienne Posta |
| Farouk | Richard Tate |
| Lord Soper | Tony Scannell |
| Mrs McGuinness | Anna Sharkey |
| Kemal | Maynard Williams |
| Rouse | Richard Tate |
| Harry | Michael G. Jones |
| Chauffeur | Bob Packham |
| Egyptian Servant | Michael G. Jones |
| Taureg | Michael G. Jones |
| Anubis | Maynard Williams |

Directed by Ken Hill
Designed by Sarah-Jane McClelland
Lighting by Ian Callender
Dances by Adrienne Posta
Musical direction, vocal and orchestral arrangements by Bunny Thompson

The play is designed to be performed by nine actors, doubling as necessary, with some extras (possibly children) and assistance from Acting A.S.M.s.

## ACT I

| | |
|---|---|
| SCENE 1 | The Palace of the High Priest, Thebes. 1380 BC |
| SCENE 2 | A Room in the British Museum, AD 1922. |
| SCENE 3 | Professor Niven's Home |
| SCENE 4 | The Egyptian Warehouse in Wapping |
| SCENE 5 | Tilbury Docks |
| SCENE 6 | Aboard the *Alexandria* |
| SCENE 7 | Kemal's Villa in Cairo |
| SCENE 8 | Aboard the Dhow |
| SCENE 9 | Ruins in the Desert |
| SCENE 10 | In the Desert above the Tomb |
| SCENE 11 | The Tomb of Inmutef-Amun |

## ACT II

| | |
|---|---|
| SCENE 1 | Ayashet's Palace |
| SCENE 2 | Below the Palace |
| SCENE 3 | A Small Chamber |
| SCENE 4 | The Base of the Well |
| SCENE 5 | The River of Life |

## MUSICAL NUMBERS

### ACT I
1. I've Got A Thing For You — Paul, Nancy
2. Oh Tilbury — Rouse, Harry
3. Sailing Away — Mrs McGuinness, Company
4. Gods Of Old — Ashayet
5. Life Is Full Of Mysteries — Paul, Nancy, Niven, Soper, Kemal, Rouse

### ACT II
6. Maturity — Ashayet, Kemal
7. British Heroes — Soper, Niven, Paul
8. Get Down — Nancy
9. Sailing Away *Reprise* — Company

## AUTHOR'S NOTE

*The Mummy's Tomb* is towards the end of a long line of similar works which first saw the light of day at Theatre Workshop, Stratford East. As one would expect, coming from such an illustrious source, it only works on a very truthful level. Any attempt to "send up" or "guy" the play or performances will result in a poor and unfunny evening's entertainment.

The pace of the play itself is very fast, otherwise it will come out very long. The scenes should "cut" into one another like a film, and any protracted scene changes or black-outs simply *must* be avoided.

Music forms an integral part of the action, colouring, heightening, relieving, pointing tension, romance, drama, danger. It is ostensibly played for some of the time by a character in the piece, seated at the piano. If a piano-playing actor (or acting pianist) is available, then excellent. If not, he can mime and it can all be doubled by an offstage piano-player, who is in any case needed for those moments the character is involved elsewhere. Both pianists, however, should resist the temptation to quote either from songs written for the piece, or well-known tunes. The emphasis must be on mood only.

The play, in its present form, contains a number of songs, the music for which is available from Samuel French Ltd. These are very simple, tuneful and easily sung, and provide a nice relief from the frenetic goings-on, but for companies who feel they are beyond their resources they can easily be cut.

The arrangements for these songs were originally for quartet of piano, bass, drums and alto saxophone doubling clarinet and flute. These arrangements are available from Theatre Royal, Stratford East.

The setting described in this acting edition worked very well and provided exactly what was required, but like all these plays *The Mummy's Tomb* is capable of being done within the simplest of scenery—or even, none at all.

## STAGING

The setting is on two levels, the higher running from R to L across the stage at a reasonable depth, and high enough for entrances to be made beneath it. The front edge of this area can be closed off by sliding panels, all of which are reversible to give various scenic backgrounds. The central part of the upstage edge of this area is also closed off by sliding panels, these always representing a rough brick wall.

All masking is in the form of relieved profiles, representing Egyptian-style pillars and decoration. Two smaller versions of these pillars form an arch with a header over the centre of the upper level.

The background is always either cyclorama or black travellers drawn in front of it.

This production was also designed around a central trap, available at the Theatre Royal, which was capable not only of providing a pit in the stage, but of elevating to form a platform. There are also some flown pieces as described in the text.

> The publication of this play in French's Acting Edition must not be taken to imply that it is available for performance. To avoid possible infringement of the copyright please read the fee notice very carefully.

# ACT I

### Scene 1
### (PROLOGUE)

*The Palace of the High Priest, Thebes—1380 BC*

*As the* Curtain *rises, a loud gong is heard, and music continues, ostensibly led by Paul Conway at the piano. The setting represents the Palace of the High Priest. Front panels* r *and* l *depict Egyptian wall paintings. The* c *panels are similarly designed, but gauzed and painted to look like sliding doors. Above, in front of the central arch, is the huge statue of a Pharaoh-God, gazing down dispassionately. The light is dim, greenish and mysterious, except for a bright spot on Paul Conway. He sits at his piano up* r, *dressed in white tuxedo, black bow tie, black trousers, playing. He looks up at us and smiles*

**Paul** Our tale has its roots in an ancient tragedy—nearly one and a half thousand years before the birth of Christ—in Egypt—at Thebes—in the Valley of the Tombs of the Kings. Here lived Inmutef-Amun, High Priest of Amun-Ra—said by some to be even more powerful a figure than Pharaoh himself—for Inmutef-Amun possessed the secret of Eternal Life!

*Gong. The gauzed* c *panels open sharply*

*Inmutef-Amun enters, dragging Selena*

**Selena** No! No!

*He flings her down* l

My lord! Please! I beg of you!
**Inmutef** It is pointless to resist me, Selena. And why should you wish to? A mere slave girl stolen from the West?
**Selena** (*on her knees*) Please, my lord!
**Inmutef** You little fool! Do you not realize what the High Priest of Amun-Ra can give in return for your love? I can make you anything you wish—my Queen—my Princess—my Wife! I can even give you Immortality.

*Chords*

**Selena** And what use is that, my lord, if it condemns me to an eternity of misery? I love another!
**Inmutef** (*in contempt*) Yes! A nonentity! A mere nobody! A Necropolis guard who even now is paying for his temerity!

*There is a horrible scream off* R. *Paul looks off, alarmed. Selena rises, goes to Inmutef and holds his hand*

**Selena** Oh please, my lord—release us! We have done you no harm!
**Inmutef** No harm? (*Flinging off her clutching hands*) You have caused me to love you, and that foolish boy has stolen you away from me! No harm? He dies . . .!
**Selena** No, my lord!
**Inmutef** Now!

*He signals off. There is another scream, and a dying gurgle. Paul puts hands hands over face and then quickly plays a tragic chord. Selena screams, covers her face and moves slowly down* L

As for you, my dear Selena—if I cannot have you willingly, then I shall have you *un*willingly! (*He puts his arm round her and draws her close*)

*Selena struggles and screams*

*The black-cloaked figure of Ashayet, carrying a knife, makes a sudden entrance* L *of the* C *panel to the* R *panel*

**Ashayet** Inmutef!

*Paul plays minor chords. Selena starts back. Inmutef turns. They slowly circle one another, Ashayet going below Inmutef to be near Selena, Inmutef going above Ashayet to end up* C. *During this, Paul plays and speaks*

**Paul** The Pharaoh's wife—who was under the impression she had a similar hold over Inmutef's affections. The eternal triangle—an institution of great antiquity.

*Ashayet stabs Inmutef. He throws back his head and laughs, quite unharmed*

**Inmutef** You poor woman! You know you cannot kill me! Come! Strike again!

*She raises the blade*

Strike!

*She turns and stabs Selena*

No!

*He runs to Selena and catches her. Ashayet crosses to the piano and puts the knife down upon it. Inmutef cradles the dying Selena in his arms*

Selena . . .!
**Selena** (*faintly*) I prefer death, my lord. (*She dies*)
**Inmutef** Oh, Selena! I shall love you through all eternity!

*Gong*

**Paul** And here's his chance! (*He indicates the* C *entrance*)

*The Pharaoh Amenhotep IV, Mahu and two Palace Guards appear. They hold a tableau for a second then move immediately to Inmutef*

## Act I, Scene 1

*Mahu picks up Selena and the two Guards grab Inmutef and begin to drag him off C. Ashayet slinks down R*

**Inmutef** What are you doing? Amenhotep! Nobody may touch the High Priest of Amun-Ra! No-one! No-one . . . !

*By now Inmutef has been dragged off R through the C entrance and Selena carried off L through the same entrance*

*The gauzed panels close before the Pharaoh speaks. Music continues throughout his speech*

**Amenhotep** Wife . . .

*Ashayet faces front*

You betray me, not only as a husband, but as a King. You and this evil breed must be stamped out for all time. For too long now has Inmutef-Amun bathed in the River of Life, for too long his this insensate god, Amun-Ra ruled in Egypt. Henceforth, the High Priest shall be a mortal man answerable only to the Great Aten, whose rays warm us all, King and commoner alike. (*Moving down* L) We cannot kill Inmutef-Amun—this we know—but we *can* condemn him to eternal life in a tomb so deep and distant that none shall ever discover its whereabouts. Behold your lover's punishment. (*He indicates the central gauzed panels*)

*Lights come up behind the gauze to reveal the struggling Inmutef. The two Guards have just completed bandaging him as a mummy and are beginning to wrap the bandages over his eyes*

**Ashayet** Inmutef! (*She runs to the gauzed panels*) Inmutef . . . !

*The Lights fade and Ashayet falls to her knees, bowing her head*

**Amenhotep** As for you—go now—without hope or attendants. Go into the Great Desert in the East. You are banished. And should you again set foot in the Valley of the Nile you shall suffer the same punishment as your lover. Go! (*He points* R)

*Ashayet goes off R slowly, behind the piano*

*Paul watches her go, still playing, then turns to face front*

**Paul** And so the living Inmutef is carried into the desert to his last resting place—a place so secret that none shall discover it for all time—a place whose secrecy is *guaranteed* . . .

*Paul stops playing and indicates the C gauzed panels, which open sharply*

*Mahu appears smartly L and meets the First Guard who comes on R— both inside the high level, beneath it*

**First Guard** It is done, my lord.
**Mahu** Are the burial party dead?
**First Guard** All dead, my lord.

**Mahu** In that case... (*He stabs the Guard who dies with a scream. He then crosses smartly down to the Pharaoh*) It is done, great lord.
**Amenhotep** Are the slaves dead?
**Mahu** (*bowing*) As you commanded, great lord.
**Amenhotep** In that case...

*He stabs Mahu, who falls across him with a scream. The Pharaoh throws him down* L *so that he is partially off stage*

You have done well, Mahu. The chain is complete. Even *I* do not know where Inmutef-Amun now rests.

*Music*

*Amenhotep sweeps round* C *and off up* L

*The Lights on the lower level fade, except for the spot on Paul. The gauzed panels close*

**Paul** (*playing*) And rest, Inmutef did—but not the Pharaoh's wife—

*Above, the hooded figure of Ashayet crosses slowly from* R *to* L *in front of the Pharaoh-God*

—for, in a moment of foolish passion, Inmutef had allowed her to bathe in the River of Life. She was now immortal, and would henceforth journey through the centuries in search of her beloved. (*He pauses*) And so—time passes...

*Paul—and the Band—play a little dignified march*

Alexander conquers the world and dies—Rome conquers a larger world and fades into oblivion...

*The Lights fade to a Black-out, and the scene is changed as Paul continues speaking*

Christ is born, dies and is resurrected. There is the march of Moslem, of Magyar, Celt, Pict, Angle and Saxon. The far sea-journeys of the Phoenicians, the Vikings, the Polynesians, the Portuguese. The Dark Ages, the Middle Ages, the Renaissance, and the building of Merchant Empires—of industrialization, of oil and coal and great ships—until finally—nearly three-and-a-half thousand years later—in the early nineteen-twenties—as the calendar is now reckoned in the land of a relative newcomer to the scene—at the British Museum...

Scene 2

*A Room in the British Museum, 1922*

*The Lights come up to reveal Professor Niven working at his desk, down* L. *He has a large magnifying glass on a string around his neck, and is carefully examining broken papyrus under glass. On the desk, near his elbow, is a Sumerian clay tablet, a Coptic knife, and various odds and ends. As Paul finishes, he folds his arms, leans back and watches*

**Nancy** (*off*) Daddy! Daddy!

*Nancy runs on, very prettily dressed in nineteen-twenties style, wearing hat, gloves, carrying a handbag*

Oh hallo, Daddy!

**Niven** Hallo, dear.

*She puts her handbag on his desk*

And *don't* get nail-varnish all over my two thousand year old papyrus!

**Nancy** Honestly, Daddy, you and your boring hairyglyphics.

**Niven** Hieroglyphs. And I've got to get this translation ready for the new exhibition in the Egyptian Room, so if you don't mind . . .

**Nancy** Now, Daddy, you know I wouldn't normally *dream* of disturbing you. It's just that I want you to meet my fiancé.

**Niven** Nancy, ever since your mother died—rest her soul and who'd know a cobra could climb stairs—I've met no fewer than fourteen of your fiancés, and I'm getting a trifle blasé about them. What does this one do?

**Nancy** He works in a theatre.

**Niven** For a *living*?

**Nancy** Well—no. But he plays a lovely piano.

*Paul goes into a short, thundering rhapsody, then sweeps back his hair, cracks his knuckles and rises*

Paul.

**Paul** (*moving* C) Delighted to meet you, Professor. Paul Conway. Nancy's told me a lot about you. Apparently you're an expert on Egyptology.

**Niven** Yes, and I'm also an expert on Nancy's fiancés. I give you— (*looking at him through the magnifying glass*)—a fortnight.

**Paul** I beg your pardon?

**Niven** Well, that's pretty good, really—the record's only three and a half weeks. Mind, that doesn't really count—he was in Singapore most of the time. Nice chap. Lord Rodney Soper.

**Nancy** Honestly, Daddy, you'll offend him. Paul knows this time he's special.

**Niven** He looks the same as all the others to me.

**Nancy** (*going to Paul, holding his hands, gazing up into his eyes*) Oh, but he's not—he's the one and only—the best chap who ever lived. Ripping all round.

**Niven** That's what I said: same as all the others.

**Farouk** (*off*) Effendi! Effendi!

*Farouk comes quickly on* R, *above the piano. He carries a huge vase very carefully*

**Niven** Dash it all, Farouk—what is it now?

**Farouk** (*with great pride*) Look!
**Niven** (*rising*) Great heavens! It's an Eighteenth-Dynasty Vase! (*Going to him*) And in a state of the uttermost preservation! (*Taking it from him, carefully*) Where under earth did you find it?

*Nancy shrugs and sits on the corner of the desk*

**Farouk** A new tomb has been discovered, and the great Lord Carnarvon has sent this for you to personally examine.
**Niven** But whose tomb is it?
**Farouk** Tutankhamun.
**Niven** Tutankhamun!
**Nancy** Tutankhamun? Never head of him.
**Niven** A rather obscure little boy-king, my dear—son of Amenhotep. This must rank as the most momentous discovery in the history of archaeology!
**Paul** Excuse me, Professor, but haven't I read somewhere there's a curse on whoever disturbs the last resting-place of a mummy?
**Niven** Fiddlesticks.
**Farouk** Forgive me, Effendi, but several bearer cousins of mine have already pegged it in somewhat mysterious circumstances, and are even now—(*taking off his fez*)—resting in the bosom of Allah.
**Niven** Poppycock. I've been digging 'em up for years and I'm as healthy as anybody. In fact, nothing unfortunate has happened whatsoever—absolutely nothing.

*Farouk gives a sudden great shivering cry and knocks the Professor's elbow. The vase falls to the ground and shatters*

Oh great heavens, what have you made me do! (*He kneels and hurriedly picks up the pieces*)
**Farouk** Forgive me, Effendi, but a terrible tingle ran right up and down my spine!

*Farouk and Paul help Niven to pick up the pieces*

**Nancy** It's all right, Daddy, it'll stick together again.
**Niven** Stick together again! It's three and a half thousand years old!
**Nancy** Well, it's just as well it wasn't a new one, dear.

*All the pieces are now collected and Niven becomes aware in a brief pause that Farouk, is examining something in his hand*

**Niven** What have you got there, Farouk?
**Farouk** (*hurriedly putting it in his pocket*) Nothing, Effendi.
**Niven** If it's a piece of the vase, give it to me (*He goes to Farouk*)
**Farouk** (*moving round and below Niven, keeping face to him*) Nothing to do with the vase, Effendi. Must have dropped from my pocket earlier.
**Niven** Give it to me.
**Farouk** (*backing to the desk*) Excuse me, Effendi, very busy. Must go now.
**Niven** Give it to me immediately!

*A brief pause*

## Act I, Scene 2

**Farouk** Never. (*Looking around him wildly*) Never!

*Farouk sees the knife on the desk, snatches it up and strikes at Niven with it. Niven grabs his uplifted arm*

**Paul** Sorry, old bean, can't be having that.

*He smartly picks up the clay tablet and hits Farouk over the head with it. It shatters and Farouk collapses*

**Niven** (*beside himself with anguish*) The earliest known Sumerian clay tablet! What are you, Conway? A raving Visigoth? (*He picks up the pieces and carefully places them on the piano*)

**Paul** (*picking up the knife*) Sorry, Professor, but he was going to stick this knife into you. (*He goes through Farouk's pockets*)

**Niven** (*snatching it*) That doesn't matter—it's only Coptic. But the clay tablet . . .! (*He puts the knife on the piano*)

**Nancy** Don't worry, Daddy . . .

**Niven** Yes, I know! Bit of putty and it'll be as right as rain!

*Paul straightens, with a round piece of pottery in his hand*

**Paul** This is what he was hanging on to. Mean anything to you, sir? (*He hands it to Niven*)

**Niven** (*uninterestedly*) What? (*Suddenly struck*) What? (*Taking out a magnifying glass and examining it*) Amazing!

**Nancy** What is it, Daddy?

**Niven** (*with great emphasis*) It's the bottom of the vase!

**Nancy** Well, I don't see anything amazing about that. I mean, if vases didn't have bottoms, they'd fall over and all the water would run out.

**Niven** (*going to her quickly*) Yes, but look *here*, dear . . .!

*He shows her the piece of pottery, Paul going behind and between them to look also*

**Nancy** Hairyglyphics.

**Niven** Hieroglyphs! But *inside*! Actually cut *inside* the vase!

**Paul** What do they say, sir? Can you translate?

**Niven** (*snapping*) Of course I can translate, Conway. What do you think I'm doing here?

*Farouk suddenly jumps to his feet and rushes down into the auditorium and out L*

**Paul** Hold on a minute there! (*He runs down after him*)

**Niven** Oh let him go. He'll know better than to show his face in the British Museum again.

**Nancy** Hear hear.

**Paul** (*returning*) Little beggar was shamming. But why did he try to steal that thing, sir? Is it valuable?

**Niven** Valuable? I should say so! It actually gives the secret of the location of the tomb of Inmutef-Amun!

*Minor chords. All start and look at the piano. Niven examines it through his magnifying glass*

**Nancy** Inmutef-Amun? Who's he?
**Niven** You mean you don't know who Inmutef-Amun is?
**Nancy** Not offhand, no.
**Niven** What did your mother and I spend all that money on your education for?
**Paul** I've never heard of him either, sir.
**Niven** Oh shut up, Conway. I didn't pay for *you* to go to Roedean. (*To Nancy*) Surely you've heard of the Pharaoh Amenhotep and his conflict with the High Priests of Amun-Ra?
**Nancy** No, Daddy.
**Niven** (*fed up*) Well, have you perhaps stumbled across Egypt? What about the continent of Africa?
**Nancy** Now don't be silly, Daddy. I know Africa as well as the next gel. It's all those silly men in turbans chasing tigers.
**Paul** I think that's India, dear.
**Niven** ⎫
**Nancy** ⎬ Shut up. ⎰ (*Speaking together*)
**Niven** Oh well, I suppose I'd better explain. You see, the main religion in Egypt for thousands of years was the worship of Amun-Ra, a kind of Sun God. But during the regin of Amenhotep, the Pharaoh fell out with his High Priest for some reason or other and began to worship a new deity called the Aten, who was a more democratic sort of a chap, as deities go.
**Nancy** Well, if you know all this already, Daddy, what's all the excitement about?
**Niven** Because, you see, nobody's ever been certain quite *why* Amenhotep broke with the old religion. All that's known for sure is that he ordered the execution of his High Priest, Inmutef-Amun, and that the man's grave was to be unmarked and far away from the normal burial grounds.
**Paul** And this piece of pottery tells you where the tomb actually *is*?
**Niven** Yes! It's the last will and testament of a Palace Guard called— (*checking through the magnifying glass*)—Mahu. The Pharaoh killed him personally so that he couldn't reveal the secret of the location, but he must have lived long enough to dictate this. And it's *been* here, concealed, unseen and unsuspected, for three and a half thousand years!
**Nancy** But I still don't understand why that little twerp Farouk would want to steal it.
**Niven** Yes, and he was even prepared to kill me for it. I don't know what's in this tomb, but it is indubitably a mystery, and a mystery that must and *shall* be solved!
**Paul** (*getting excited himself and moving to Niven*) So what are you going to do about it, sir?
**Niven** (*clapping him on the shoulder*) Go there, my boy! What else? I may not be able to rival Tutankhamun, but I can certainly knock some of the gilt off the gingerbread. I'm off to my rooms to pack immediately!

*Niven goes off quickly* R *above the piano*

## Act I, Scene 2

**Paul** Professor . . . !

*Paul half goes to follow him, then stops by the piano. Nancy rises*

**Nancy** Poor old Daddy. He can't go exploring again at his age.

**Paul** (*sitting at the piano*) Do you know, I'd give my eye teeth to go on an expedition like that! (*He plays a chord*)

**Nancy** That's because you've never *been* on one. I've been dragged halfway across the world since I was so high. (*She indicates*)

**Paul** Then why didn't you know where Africa was?

**Nancy** Because when you've seen one dusty fly-ridden continent, you've seen the lot really. I never cared *where* I was. In fact . . .

*Music from the Band: flute and bells. Nancy stops and shivers*

**Paul** What's the matter, dear?

**Nancy** I don't know. It was as though somebody walked over my grave. I suddenly felt I knew a great deal about this Inmutef-Amun—far more than I actually do.

**Paul** Honestly! What an imaginative little hen you are! (*Playing*) We're going to be so happy together.

**Nancy** (*going to the desk and leaning against it*) Not unless you stop calling me names, we're not.

**Paul** (*still playing*) I shall *always* call you names. Beautiful names. (*He sings as he plays*)

### SONG 1: I've Got A Thing For You

    I've got a thing for you
    Say you've got a thing for me
    Let's put our things together
    And see whether we can agree

**Nancy** Life is no fun for one
    Love was intended for two
    As Jack said to Jill
    As they climbed up the hill
    I've got a thing for you

*Paul indicates to the Band that they should take over for him, rises and meets Nancy* C

**Paul**    Oh, Nancy, you're my fancy
        You're the one that I adore

**Nancy**  Oh, Paul, to me, you're all a man should be
        And something more

**Paul**    Sweetie, always treat me, to your kisses
        I implore
        To say the least, you bring out the beast
        In me forever more

*Dance break. They dance together, finishing* C *again*

| | |
|---|---|
| Nancy | Oh, dearest, stay the nearest |
| | Please don't ever tell me no |
| Paul | Oh honey, it's so funny |
| | But I think I'm all aglow |
| Both | Hold me and enfold me in your arms |
| | Don't let me go |
| Nancy | That Cupid's not so stupid |
| | He's just shot us with his bow |
| | So |

*They dance and sing*

| | |
|---|---|
| | I've got a feel for you |
| Paul | I've got a feel for you |
| Nancy | Say you've got a feel for me |
| Paul | You've got a feel for me |
| Nancy | Sweetheart, let's feel |
| Both | Together |
| | And blue skies forever we'll see |
| Nancy | Happy we two, side by side |
| Paul | We're happy, side by side |
| Nancy | We're at heaven's gate |
| Both | Let's walk through |
| | As Darby told Joan |
| | Every night on their own |
| | I've got a thing for you. |

*They finish, Nancy sitting on Paul's knee, below the piano,* R

*Lord Soper enters up* L, *wearing overcoat, scarf and hat*

**Lord Soper** Aha!

*Paul and Nancy break apart, Nancy on the inside*

**Nancy** Rodney!
**Lord Soper** (*snatching off his hat*) So its *true*! Gad, Nancy, you and I swore everlasting affection just before I went to Singapore. I've only been gone a week!
**Paul** Who is this man?
**Nancy** Erm—Lord Rodney Soper—Mr Paul Conway.
**Lord Soper** }
**Paul** } Her fiancé! Her *what*? { (*Speaking together*)
**Paul** (*arms folded, facing front*) Do you mean to say you're engaged to *both* of us, Nancy? Didn't you tell him about *me*?
**Nancy** Well—Rodney's very sensitive. I was going to drop him a card when I was sure.
**Lord Soper** Drop me a card!
**Paul** When you were sure!
**Lord Soper** (*moving to the desk*) Oh, if only I had a gun!...
**Paul** Oh now, hold on, your lordship—!
**Lord Soper** Not for *you*, you blithering idiot! Who'd want to shoot a little

## Act I, Scene 2

pipsqueak like you? You're not worth the bullet. (*Dropping brokenly into Niven's chair*) No, its *me*! It would be for *me*.

**Nancy** (*patting him*) Poor Rodney. (*To Paul, angrily*) I told you he was sensitive!

*Paul fumes*

**Lord Soper** I'll just have to go abroad again, to forget—though God knows, I'm getting heartily sick of it. After Lady Beryl, I went up the Amazon and got a poisoned arrow in me liver. After the Honourable Georgina Ward, I went up the Orinoco, and got bitten by a bird-eating spider. And after Fifi Blanquette, I went up the Red River and got Yellow Fever. It's too too much, Nancy.

**Nancy** Well, it won't be anywhere near as bad this time. (*Going to Paul*) He can go up the Nile with Daddy.

**Paul** What?

*Lord Soper rises, nervously*

**Nancy** He needs somebody to pay for the trip.

**Lord Soper** (*apprehensively*) The Nile? That's crocodiles, isn't it?

**Paul** (*grimly*) Yes—big ones.

**Nancy** Yes, but I'm sure you'll survive somehow. (*Going to Lord Soper*) So why don't you go and talk to him? He's at home.

**Lord Soper** Yes, well, I suppose it would take my mind off things.

**Nancy** (*going to the desk*) Yes, it would, dear. (*She sits on the edge and sorts through her handbag. After a pause*) Well, what's keeping you?

**Lord Soper** Is this fellow staying here?

**Paul** I certainly am.

**Nancy** You certainly are not. You have to go to the theatre and play your piano.

**Lord Soper** (*scornfully amused*) Piano-player?

**Paul** (*looking at his watch*) Good Lord, you're right! I'm late! (*He moves to the piano, begins to push it off* R, *then pauses and turns on Lord Soper*) Are you coming or not?

**Lord Soper** After you.

**Paul** No, after *you*, my lord.

**Lord Soper** After you, you little . . .

**Nancy** (*sharply*) Oh go on—both of you!

*Paul and Lord Soper go off* R, *Paul pushing the piano, Lord Soper carrying the stool*

*Nancy makes up, using the compact from her handbag. The Lights begin to dim*

Honestly—men! They make mountains out of molehills. I mean, so long as one's married, who cares who to?

*Minor music*

*Farouk comes on up* L, *sinisterly casual, and wanders behind Nancy*

*Nancy sees him in the mirror of her compact*

Farouk! What are you . . . ?

*Farouk grabs her and puts a cloth over her mouth. She struggles a moment, then becomes limp*

*Smiling malevolently, Farouk drags Nancy off* R

*The Lights fade to a small area* C. *The arguing voices of Lord Soper and Niven are heard over the scene change*

Scene 3

*Professor Niven's Home. Night*

*Mrs McGuinness makes an immediate entrance, pushing a trolley to* LC, *followed by the arguing Niven and Lord Soper. Niven crosses to* RC *and Lord Soper follows him up* C. *As they enter, the ad lib argument terminates*

**Niven** Yes, but look here, Lord Soper, this is a serious business! Apart from the Nile, Egypt's all desert—no water for hundreds of miles—blazing heat—sandstorms—It's no joy ride, my boy.
**Mrs McGuinness** Excuse me, Professor, you'll be wanting your dinner now.
**Niven** Please, Mrs McGuinness, don't bother me.
**Lord Soper** I insist upon coming on this expedition, Professor! (*Moving* C, *his back to the trolley*) Damn it all, your daughter's just broken my heart!
**Niven** If I took everybody she did *that* to, I'd need a camel train half a mile long! It's just not on, your lordship.
**Mrs McGuinness** It's your favourite, Professor—cockyleeky flambé. (*She ignites the omelette pan, which goes off with a big whoosh, singeing the back of Lord Soper's trousers*)
**Lord Soper** You blithering idiot!
**Niven** Mrs McGuinness—please! (*To Lord Soper*) The answer is no, Lord Soper. I shall go alone.
**Lord Soper** And how will you pay for it?
**Niven** Well, I shall—erm—I shall . . .
**Mrs McGuinness** You'll speak to the Royal Society, Professor.
**Niven** I shall speak to the Royal Society. In fact, I have already done so and am expecting their call at any minute.

*The telephone rings, to Niven's surprise*

**Mrs McGuinness** That will be them now, sir. (*She goes off* L *and returns with the telephone on a tray. She brings it between them and answers it*)
**Niven** (*during this*) You see? So if you don't mind . . .

## Act I, Scene 3

*Farouk enters on the upper level R carrying a telephone*

**Lord Soper** I think I'll just stay and here what they have to say—if *you* don't mind.

**Mrs McGuinness** (*on the telephone*) Professor Niven's residence.

**Niven** Give that to *me*, Mrs McGuinness. (*Snatching it*) Niven here.

*A spot picks out the figure of Farouk, his back to us*

**Farouk** Good evening, Effendi. I trust you know who this is?

**Niven** Farouk?

**Farouk** (*turning front*) Yes—Farouk—the little gyppy servant you bullied for the past two years. But all that will now cease.

**Niven** What do you want, Farouk?

**Farouk** The location of the tomb of Inmutef-Amun.

**Niven** Are you mad?

**Farouk** In exchange for your daughter's life.

**Niven** What? (*To Lord Soper*) He's got Nancy.

**Lord Soper** What, *another* blessed fiancé?

**Niven** No—he's kidnapped her.

**Lord Soper** Give that phone to me. (*He snatches it and speaks*) Lord Soper here. Now what is all this . . .

**Farouk** Just bring me the map—to the Egyptian Warehouse in Wapping—before eleven o'clock tonight—otherwise, you will never see Miss Niven alive again.

**Lord Soper** (*on the telephone*) Now look here . . .

*Farouk slams down his telephone and carries it off*

By George, the little swine means it. Who is he, anyway?

*He gives the telephone back to Mrs McGuinness, who takes it off and returns with Niven's clothes*

**Niven** (*taking off his cardigan*) I'll explain on the way. Oh, and we'd better pick up Conway too.

*Mrs McGuinness helps him into his hat, coat and scarf*

**Lord Soper** Conway? What the dickens do we need *him* for?

**Niven** Well, after all, the poor devil *is* engaged to her!

**Lord Soper** He's not the only one. *You* pick up Conway. I'll get to the warehouse first.

*Lord Soper goes off L. Niven follows*

**Mrs McGuinness** (*going down to her trolley*) Does all this mean there'll only be two for dinner tonight, Professor?

**Niven** (*sticking his head back in*) This is no time for trifles, Mrs McGuinness!

*Niven goes*

**Mrs McGuinness** It's a blancmange, Professor.

*Lord Soper sticks his head back in*

**Lord Soper** Mrs McGuinness, where *is* Wapping?
**Mrs McGuinness** Oh Lord Soper, I'm sure I don't know! . . .

*Lord Soper goes and then enters during the Black-out*

*Mrs McGuinness grumbles to herself, wheeling the trolley off, as the Lights fade to a Black-out. Whispered voices are heard off as the scene changes*

SCENE 4

*The Egyptian Warehouse in Wapping*

*The sound of lapping water and foghorns is heard. The whole of the beginning of the scene is played in a Black-out with only torchlight, so the following dialogue begins immediately and continues over the set change*

*Paul enters down* L

**Paul** (*whispering*) Come along, Professor.
**Niven** (*off*) I'm right behind you, Conway.
**Paul** This is the warehouse all right, but there's no sign of Nancy. (*He moves his torch around auditorium*) In fact, there's nobody here at all. (*His torch picks out Lord Soper's face and he turns away quickly, screaming*) Aaagh!

*Niven runs on down* L

**Niven** What was that?
**Paul** Me going aaagh!
**Niven** This is no time for footling jokes, Conway! Ssh!
**Paul** (*dropping to a whisper again*) There's something awful in the corner over there. I just caught a glimpse of it. It was horrible. I think it was some kind of hideous Egyptian statue.
**Lord Soper** It was *me*, Conway.
**Niven** Oh there you are, Soper. (*He crosses Paul and shines torch into Lord Soper's face*) Aaaagh!
**Paul** See what I mean?
**Niven** Ssh!
**Lord Soper** (*moving down a little*) This place is like a blasted rabbit warren.
**Niven** Any sign of anybody?
**Lord Soper** No. As far as I can tell, the whole place is deserted.
**Niven** I suggest we split up and search it, then. You that way, Lord Soper—(*down into the auditorium* L)—where that sinister gurgling noise is coming from. You that way, Conway—(*in the gap under the level* R)—

## Act I, Scene 4

where the shadows keep moving about. I'll just pop off over here. (*Up* L) And pray God we're in time.

*Niven, Lord Soper and Paul scout off to their separate exits to minor chords*

*The central wall panels open sharply to* R *and* L, *and a pool of light comes up* C *and below the elevated area. Nancy is revealed, gagged and bound to a chair.*

*Farouk strides in,* LC, *looking at his watch*

**Farouk** It is way past the deadline. Where is that crazy father of yours? I will kill you if he doesn't come. I will. Just like that. Surely he does not value the map more than your life. He must come, I tell you! Soon the other man will be arriving. He must want the map very badly to pay me so much money. Rich at last! But what if I don't have it for him? Allah be merciful, what will he do to me? (*Turning on her*) It's all your father's fault! He despises me! He thinks I don't have the courage! Well, I know I have! I think ... Yes, I have!

*A clock begins to strike twelve*

Twelve o'clock! The fool! Your father! He's gone to the police!

*Nancy desperately struggles and shakes her head*

Oh yes he has! Well, I'm sorry, pretty lady, but its every man for himself in this life!

*He puts a hand behind the wall* L *and mimes pulling a lever. The trap in the stage opens. Sinister gurgling of water and a green glow comes from it*

It's into the river with you and run like hell, Farouk. (*He picks her up*) And it's no use struggling. I'm a very strong little chap. (*He goes to throw her down the trap*) One and a two and a ...

*Lord Soper and Paul rush on at the same time, Lord Soper from up* L, *Paul from up* R

**Lord Soper** ⎱ Oh no you don't! Stay out of this ⎱
**Paul** ⎰ Conway (Soper), *I'm* rescuing ⎰ (*Speaking together*)
Nancy, not you.

**Farouk** (*putting Nancy down and beaming*) Hallo, Effendi.
**Paul** Farouk you bounder! (*Adopting a fighting pose*) Put up your dukes!
**Farouk** (*moving towards Lord Soper,* L *of the trap*) Oh please—this man— he will damage me. (*Putting up his hands*) Look! I surrender!
**Lord Soper** Sopers don't take prisoners. (*He produces a gun and shoots Farouk*)

*Farouk gives a cry and falls into the trap. His echoing, falling voice is heard—fading*

**Farouk** (*off*) The curse of the Black Scorpion be upon you-ooh ...!

*Splash. Nancy mumbles through her gag. Both hastily release her and take her down* R

**Lord Soper** } Are you all right, darling? { (*Speaking together*)
**Paul**

*They glare at each other*

**Nancy** Yes, I think so. But it was horrible—horrible! (*She sobs on Lord Soper's chest*)
**Lord Soper** (*patting her head, smiling triumphantly at Paul*) Most horrible.
**Nancy** (*looking up, seeing she is on the wrong chest, and speaking to Paul*) Oh. Sorry. (*Sobbing on Paul's chest*) Horrible! Horrible!

*Niven comes on down* L

**Niven** Nancy! Thank heavens you're safe. Your poor dear mother would never have forgiven me.
**Nancy** (*moving to him*) Oh, Daddy, it was horrible—horrible!
**Lord Soper** I suggest we get out of this filthy place.
**Niven** Good thinking, Soper.
**Paul** (*moving to Nancy and taking her hands in his*) Don't worry, Nancy—we've got you back.
**Lord Soper** *And* we've still got the map.
**Niven** (*moving to him*) Yes, and I'll tell you one thing—nobody's ever going to wrest it from me. Oh, by the way—what's happened to Farouk?
**Lord Soper** Ah.
**Niven** Oh.
**Lord Soper** Yes.
**Niven** (*taking off his hat*) Ah.
**Lord Soper** Mind you, he didn't strike me as being the sort of chap capable of planning a caper like this.
**Paul** No, but somebody certainly did.

*Kemal appears rather mysteriously in the* C *entrance, from* R, *wearing fedora, camel-hair overcoat slung negligently over his shoulders and smoking a cigarette in a holder*

**Lord Soper** And if *he* didn't do it . . .
**Niven** Who *did*?
**Kemal** Good evening.

*They all jump out of their skins. Music is heard: flute and bells—an eastern flavour*

Forgive me. (*Moving down* C *and stepping over the trap as if it was not there*) I did not wish to cause any concern.
**Nancy** (*crying out a warning and taking a step towards him*) Ah—(*realizing he is now safe*)—that's quite all right. I'm sure it was our fault completely.

*Kemal glances back casually at the trap. Nancy is completely smitten with him—a fact that does not go unnoticed by Lord Soper and Paul*

**Lord Soper** And who the devil are you, sir?
**Kemal** My name is Kemal.

## Act II, Scene 4

**Nancy** (*adoring the name*) Kemal!

*Seeing the danger, Lord Soper and Paul go to Nancy and drag her R, near Niven*

**Paul** And what are you doing here?
**Kemal** (*strolling* DR) That is my question, gentlemen—and lady. This is *my* warehouse.
**Lord Soper** Your warehouse! . . .
**Nancy** ⎫
**Paul** ⎬ It's *his* warehouse! . . . (*Speaking together*)
**Niven** ⎭
**Lord Soper** And what time did *you* arrive this evening?
**Kemal** I have just walked through the door. I was passing and observed the light. I wondered if I might have burglars.

*They scoff and laugh at this notion*

Apparently I *do*.
**Niven** Good heavens, Kemal, we're not burglars! We're—we're . . .
**Lord Soper** ⎫ We're in the retail trade . . .
**Paul** ⎭ We're in the wholesale trade . . . (*Speaking together*)
**Paul** Just browsing . . .
**Nancy** (*moving towards Kemal*) Seeing if there's anything that takes our fancy . . .
**Kemal** And *does* it—
**Nancy** (*eyeing him*) Well . . .
**Kemal** —Miss Niven?

*Minor chords. Nancy reacts away from him and rejoins the group*

**Nancy** He *knows* me!
**Lord Soper** ⎫
**Paul** ⎬ He *knows* her! (*Speaking together*)
**Niven** ⎭
**Kemal** Only as the daughter of the famous Professor Niven.
**Lord Soper** ⎫
**Paul** ⎬ He knows *you!* (*Speaking together*)
**Nancy** ⎭
**Niven** Naturally.
**Kemal** Of course. I am responsible for shipping most of your antiquities from Egypt, Professor. I have often seen you from a distance at the Museum.
**Niven** Really?
**Kemal** In fact, I assume that is why you have come to see me—about the *Alexandria*.
**Nancy** The *Alexandria*?
**Kemal** The ship I have sailing tomorrow—for Karnak.
**Niven** (*excitedly*) You have a ship sailing for Karnak tomorrow? By all that's wonderful!
**Nancy** Where's Karnak?

**Niven** (*turning to her*) It's down the Nile, dear. In the Valley of... (*Going closer and lowering his voice*) In the Valley of the Tombs of the Kings. Not far from... (*He pats his pocket*)
**Kemal** If it's passage you want, Professor, I'm sure I can accommodate you. Although only a freighter, she has a few cabins.
**Lord Soper** You'd do that for us?
**Kemal** Certainly.
**Paul** (*suspiciously*) What for?
**Kemal** A thousand pounds.

*The others react*

After all, I *am* a business man.
**Niven** But I can't afford *that*! I haven't *got* a thousand pounds!
**Lord Soper** No, but *I* have. (*Going to Kemal, taking wad of notes from his wallet*) Allow me, old sport. (*Turning back to Niven*) On condition that I come with you, of course.
**Niven** Oh, I don't know about that... (*Catching Nancy's eye and seeing her nod vigorously*) Oh very well, I agree. You can come with us.

*Lord Soper gives the money to Kemal who moves away to count it*

**Nancy** Me too, Daddy! (*She skips across between Kemal and Lord Soper*)
**Niven** What, Nancy? *You?*
**Nancy** Well, you don't think I'm staying behind after all that's happened, do you?
**Lord Soper** You're coming as well, darling! Jolly dee!
**Paul** Now hold on a minute! If *he* goes, and *he* goes and *she* goes, then *I* go!
**Niven** Is that possible, Kemal?
**Kemal** All things are possible, Professor—if Allah wills. Be ready. We sail from Tilbury at dawn.

*Kemal salaams and goes off down* L

*The others attempt to respond, Nancy curtsying. Lord Soper moves down, looking after Kemal*

**Nancy** (*romantically*) Tilbury at dawn! (*Down to earth*) What a revolting idea.
**Niven** Come on, everybody! We'd better hurry off and pack.

*Niven, Paul and Nancy begin to make their way off up* R, *but are halted by Lord Soper's voice*

**Lord Soper** I say—you don't find all this rather—convenient—do you?
**Paul** What do you mean?
**Lord Soper** As though we're being rushed along somehow—given no time to think.
**Niven** Yes, that had occurred to me. And there's another thing—who *is* behind all this?
**Nancy** Oh, who cares? I'm off to pack lots of lovely frocks!
**Lord Soper** Me, too!

## Act I, Scene 5

*Nancy reacts*

Not like that, darling. I'll have to get my man to press my new safari suit.

*Lord Soper takes Nancy by the arm and draws her off quickly up R, followed by Niven*

*Paul goes to follow them, but looks at his watch as he does so*

**Paul** Oh blast! (*As he goes off up* R) I've got to go back to the theatre and finish my job.

*Paul exits*

*During the following exchange, heard off, the scene change occurs*

(*off*) See you at the docks in the morning!
**Niven** (*off*) See you at the docks, my boy—see you at the docks.
**Lord Soper** (*off*) Where *is* Tilbury, anyway?
**Nancy** (*off*) Oh shut up, Rodney!

## Scene 5

*Tilbury Docks. A bright, cold morning*

*A hooter and seagull cries are heard*

*Rouse comes on on the upper level, carrying a bollard, and singing. During the first part of the song he sets the bollard* R, *goes back, brings on a big warp line which runs off very high* L *and drops over the bollard. Harry, a dockworker, comes on at stage level up* L, *carrying a ladder, which he fits to the front face of the elevated area,* LC

### SONG 2: Oh Tilbury

**Rouse** Oh, Tilbury
Drab and unromantic
You're there with me wherever I roam
Through the foam
Oh Tilbury
Out in the Atlantic
You're every seaman's pipe-dream of home

Hull may be more pretty
Harwich—wot a city
Dover's itty-bitty
It's a pity but it's true

**Harry** Grimsby's got the glamour
Cromer needs an 'ammer
**Both** But it makes me stammer
When I think of you.

*The Band plays an orchestral verse as Harry climbs up the ladder to Rouse*

**Harry** (*speaking*) Morning, Nobby.
**Rouse** Morning, Harry. (*He takes a deep appreciative breath*)
**Harry** Hey, you like it here at Tilbury, don't you?
**Rouse** What? I mean, its my favourite dock. Just you smell that effluvia. (*Taking in a further deep breath*) Pure nectar.

*He continues singing, he and Harry walking* R

Oh, Tilbury
The oil upon your water
Adds a sort of colourful sheen
**Both** To the scene
**Rouse** Oh, Tilbury
Revered in every quarter
Of all the dingy docks you're the queen

**Harry** Dartford drives me dotty
Liverpool is grotty

*Rouse nearly knots him for this*

Bristol's full of snotty
Girls who don't come free

**Rouse** Folkestone often varies
Portsmouth's full of fairies
Yarmouth's fun but there is
Only one for me.
(*Speaking*) Shall we?

*They take hands and dance as they sing*

**Both** Oh, Tilbury
Drab and unromantic
You're there with me wherever I roam
Through the foam
Oh, Tilbury
Out in the Atlantic
You're every seaman's pipe-dream of home
Every seaman's pipe-dream
**Harry** Of home
**Rouse** Oh, Tilbury.

*They carry on with their work*

*Nancy comes on below to* C, *followed by Mrs McGuinness, Niven, and Lord Soper. Nancy is dressed in a very pretty sailor suit, Mrs McGuinness*

## Act II, Scene 5

*is wearing hat and coat and carries two large pieces of luggage, Niven is dressed in his long khaki shorts, khaki shirt, straw hat, mapcase and binoculars around his neck, also carrying two pieces of luggage, Lord Soper is dressed in a cream safari suit, with solatopi, crossed bandoliers of cartridges, a pistol at his belt, a rifle in his hand, a pack and a spare rifle in a case on his back*

**Nancy** Honestly, Daddy! Where on earth are we?
**Niven** (*putting down the luggage* RC *and sitting on it*) Don't ask me, dear. I haven't the faintest idea.

*Mrs McGuinness puts her luggage down* C

**Rouse** Oy—youse down there! What you doing in the dry dock?
**Lord Soper** What did he say?
**Niven** Well, roughly translated, what is our present purpose in these precincts?
**Harry** You can't mess about down there, mate. We're getting it ready to scrape off the *Aquitania*.
**Lord Soper** We're looking for the *Alexandria*!
**Harry** (*to Rouse*) That's yours, ain't it, Nobby?
**Rouse** Yeah, I'm a deck-hand on her. But listen, if you want to board her, you'll have to climb this here ladder now.
**Nancy** (*looking off up* L) I say, Daddy! Isn't she beautiful? Look at that big funnel and all the flags!
**Harry** That's the Royal Yacht, miss.
**Rouse** The *Alex* is the one next to it and down a bit.
**Lord Soper** What, that old tramp? Doesn't look as though it'll even go.
**Mrs McGuinness** Oh, it'll go right enough, Lord Soper—straight to the bottom.
**Niven** Now, Mrs McGuinness, stop being such a prophet of doom. We ate your blasted breakfast—what more do you want? (*To Lord Soper*) By the way, Soper, I've been meaning to ask you—why are you weighed down with all this artillery? Are you expecting trouble?
**Lord Soper** (*moving* L) One never knows with these fuzzie-wuzzies. Pot a couple of the blighters early on and they tend to respect you.

*Paul comes on up* L, *carrying a white carrier bag, and wearing a scarf and a little cap, but apart from this, in his usual clothes*

**Paul** Morning.
**Nancy** Paul! (*She runs to him and kisses him*)
**Lord Soper** I must say you're hardly dressed in suitable attire for the desert, Conway.
**Paul** Sorry, but I've been working all night. No servant to help me change. No time to even sleep.
**Nancy** (*thoughtfully, moving slowly down* C) You know, *I* didn't sleep much last night, either.
**Mrs McGuinness** Didn't you, Miss Nancy?
**Nancy** I had the most extraordinary dream . . .

*Music: flute and bells, as before*

I was lying in the dark—I couldn't move. My hands and feet seemed bound somehow. I couldn't see—my head was bound too. But I could think and I could dream. And I'd been there—I'd *been* there . . . !

*The music changes, eastern and more romantic. Nancy throws off the mood when she sees who is approaching up* L

I say!

**Lord Soper** (*who is standing in her line of sight and thinks she is referring to him*) What is it, darling? Do you like the suit? I got it in . . . (*He turns and looks off up* L) Oh. (*Disgusted, he crosses* L *of Paul*)

*Kemal enters up* L. *He has shed the hat and the overcoat, and is followed by a liveried Chauffeur, carrying his luggage*

**Kemal** Allah wills that we meet again.

*He holds out his hands and Nancy goes to him. He kisses her hands*

So it is written, so shall it be. (*He speaks in Arabic gibberish to the Chauffeur, ordering him to put down the luggage*)

**Chauffeur** Right, guv. (*He puts down the luggage up* L)
**Kemal** You have everything you need, Professor?
**Niven** Of course. This isn't the first expedition I've been on, you know.
**Nancy** Actually, Mr Kemal—I was thinking—long voyage—perhaps I could pop up to your cabin occasionally—you could help me with my hairyglyphics.
**Niven** Hieroglyphs!
**Nancy** Daddy seems to think I'm a bit rusty.
**Kemal** It will be a great pleasure.

*Kemal takes Nancy down* L, *murmuring softly to her*

**Lord Soper** (*to Paul*) There's something about that fellow sticks in my craw.
**Paul** I wonder if it's the same thing that's sticking in mine.
**Lord Soper** I wouldn't like to say.

*There is the loud blast of a ship's hooter*

**Rouse** Better get a move on, Mr Kemal, sir. The Captain won't want to miss the tide.
**Kemal** Very well, Mr Rouse—make all preparations to sail.
**Rouse** Aye aye, sir. (*Moving down* L *and calling off*) All right, George . . .

*The Party begin to pick up their luggage*

**Mrs McGuinness** Oh, Professor!
**Niven** Now now, Mrs McGuinness, don't start the waterworks. We'll be back in a couple of years.
**Mrs McGuinness** I know, sir, I know. I just can't help it.
**Niven** Oh, and don't forget to dress up in my clothes and talk to the cat occasionally. She'll forget me, otherwise.

## Act I, Scene 5

**Mrs McGuinness** I will, sir, I will.

*They begin to make their way to the ladder but are interrupted as Mrs McGuinness sings*

### SONG 3: Sailing Away

Goodbye, dear friends, I'll miss you
For parting's sweet sorrow indeed
I'll wave farewell and kiss you
And wish you good luck and Godspeed

*They begin to move off to the ladder again, but she has not finished*

I'll lay a place upon the table
Each night till you return
I'll wear a smile if I am able
But all the time I'll yearn

*They think she has finished THIS time and begin to move to the ladder, but she has not. Resigned, Niven and Paul sit on the Luggage, The Chauffeur sits on his, Lord Soper leans against the ladder*

Remember I'll be with you
Though you may be so far away
Goodbye, dear friends, I'll miss you
Till you come home some day

*This time she has finished and the others sing cheerfully as they pass luggage up to the top level, mount the ladder, wave good-bye to Mrs McGuinness, etc.*

**The Company** (*except Nancy and Mrs McGuinness*)

The siren is a-blowin'
The adrenalin is flowin'
We're sailin' away
Sailin' away
Off to sandy places
In search of an oasis to stay
The wake behind us bubbles
Like smoke our cares and troubles
Are trailin' away
Trailin' away
Cruisin' down the delta
You can swelter
As you're sailin' away.

*Mrs McGuinness faces front down R and she and Nancy sing their verse simultaneously as the Company sing their part. By the end of the song, the travellers have all left the upper level L, taking luggage with them and Harry has made his way down the ladder to the stage level*

**Mrs McGuinness** ⎫ Goodbye, dear friends, I'll miss you
**Nancy** ⎭ For parting's sweet sorrow indeed
I'll wave farewell and kiss you
And wish you good luck and Godspeed
Remember I'll be with you
Though you may be so far away
Goodbye, dear friends, I'll miss you
Til you come home some day
You come home some day
You come home some day
You come home some day

**The Company** (*singing simultaneously with Nancy and Mrs McGuinness*)
The siren is a-blowin'
The adrenalin is flowin'
We're sailin' away
Sailin' away
Off to sandy places
In search of an oasis to stay
The wake behind us bubbles
Like smoke our cares and troubles
Are trailin' away
Trailin' away
Cruisin' down the delta
You can swelter
As you're sailin' away
Cruisin' down the delta
You can swelter
As you're sailin' away
Cruisin' down the delta
You can swelter
As you're sailin' away.

**Harry** (*removing the ladder and putting it off up* L) Don't worry, darling. They'll be home before you know it. Two years ain't so very long.

**Mrs McGuinness** Oh it's a very long time, indeed it is, sir

**Harry** (*moving to her*) Here. How about you and me popping down to the *Pig and Whistle* and having a little bit of what you fancy?

**Mrs McGuinness** I wouldn't say no to a drop of the hard stuff, sir. (*Moving up* C *and peering off up* L) Oh pray God they'll be all right in that terrible old tub!

*The stage darkens. A thunderous storm rises*

**Harry** Look out, it's coming on to rain!

*Protecting Mrs McGuinness, Harry rushes off with her up* L

Act I, Scene 6                                                                                          25

## Scene 6

*Aboard the "Alexandria"*

*As Mrs McGuinness and Harry rush off up* L *two A.S.M.s, dressed in oilskins and sou'westers and carrying a length of ship's railing, made out of thin line and thin wooden uprights, rush on from up* R *to down* C. *They kneel, pulling the length of railing taut across the front of the stage, and begin to sway up and down stage, as the ship. They are closely followed by Kemal who is also dressed in oilskins and sou'wester and carries a ship's wheel. He takes a position close to the rail,* R, *facing in profile* L. *For the scene to work, actors should time the swaying of the ship to ship's rail, should not go too far away from it upstage and should play as much in profile looking* L— *the direction of travel—as possible. Because of very dim light in this small area, the stage management are able to strike the bollard and warp line and set the pillars and header upstage more or less unseen. The storm is very loud. Niven staggers on from up* R, *holding on to his hat and passes between wheel and ship's rail to* L

**Niven** (*shouting*) Where's the Captain?
**Kemal** (*shouting*) Checking the cargo. Something seems to have broken loose.

*Lord Soper staggers on up* R, *holding on to his topi, passing between the ship's rail and the wheel to* LC

**Lord Soper** (*shouting*) Ah, there you are. What's our position?
**Kemal** Desperate. She's too old for this sort of sea.
**Lord Soper** Well, good God, man, let's take to the lifeboats, then!
**Kemal** Lifeboats? What do you think you're on? The *Queen Mary*?
**Lord Soper**  ⎫
**Niven**         ⎬ No lifeboats! { (*Speaking together*)

*Paul staggers on up* R, *coat over his head, holding aloft a tray with mugs on it, and passes between ship's rail and wheel to* C

**Paul** Eight bells—time for elevenses.
**Niven** Good man, Conway. (*Taking a mug*) By the way, where's Nancy?
**Lord Soper** (*taking a mug*) Oh, she was feeling a little dicky, so I tucked her up in her bunk.
**Paul** You did *what*? (*He grabs Lord Soper's shoulder who promptly spills scalding cocoa on his hand and has to hang on to the ship's rail*) You bounder, Soper! You knew perfectly well I was making the cocoa and you took advantage of the situation!
**Lord Soper** Don't you seek to criticize *me*, you trite little theatrical!
**Niven** Gentlemen, gentlemen.
**Kemal** Gentlemen! It's easing off, I think!

*The sound of storm checks down. The Lights brighten just perceptibly*

  Mr Rouse!

**Rouse** (*off*) Coming up, sir.

*Rouse runs on up R*

**Kemal** Take the wheel.
**Rouse** Aye aye, sir.

*Rouse takes the wheel from Kemal. If the actors work it out correctly, the wheel itself will not move. Kemal comes down LC between Paul and Lord Soper, taking out a telescope and peering off down L*

**Kemal** Yes, I think we're going to be all right.
**Lord Soper** Well, thank God for that.

*Brief pause*

**Paul** Look out! There's a great big rock dead ahead!

*Rouse heaves at the wheel and all stagger a little upstage and then stagger back down to the rail. Kemal rounds on Paul*

**Kemal** It's Gibraltar.
**Lord Soper** You blithering idiot, Conway. We're supposed to go through here. But listen, Professor—this boat's too big for the Nile Delta. What happens next?
**Kemal** We go overland by rail from Alexandria to Cairo. There we can stay for a few days in my villa.
**Niven** Excellent news. We'll look forward to that. To our cabins, gentlemen.

*Niven, Paul and Lord Soper weave off up R, passing above the wheel, but keeping close to it, leaving Kemal and Rouse alone for a moment*

**Kemal** You will be coming to Cairo with me, Mr Rouse. (*He goes up R*)
**Rouse** Cairo, it is, sir. (*Brief pause*) Good old Cairo!

*Bazaar music is heard, with cries and voices chattering*

*Rouse runs off up L, and the two A.S.M.s run off down L with the ship's rail*

*The Lights come up full and warm as the scene changes*

## Scene 7

*Kemal's Villa in Cairo*

*A large Egyptian Servant, in baggy pants, bare chest and waistcoat, comes on up L, carrying a large palm tree in a pot—at least above head height, which he places up L and begins to dust with a feather duster. As he does so, Lord Soper, Niven and Paul appear up stage of the upper level from R, as far up stage as possible. The Professor carries a large old-fashioned camera on a tripod, Lord Soper a fly whisk, and Paul a small carpet, a strange easternlooking stringed instrument, and various other odds and ends that he has been persuaded to buy. They have been to the Bazaar and are still being* pestered by a lot of small Arab Children who take absolutely no notice of their efforts to drive them away

**Lord Soper** (*his voice rising out of the general chatter*) What on earth do you have to do to get rid of the horrible little urchins?
**Servant** Hey! Baksheesh! (*He throws coins through the open entrance and off upstage of the high level* R)

*The Children run off and vanish. The Servant then goes off up* R

*Lord Soper, Niven and Paul come down through the entrance into the "courtyard" of Kemal's villa*

**Niven** Thank heavens for that. We were getting a little inundated, I'm afraid.
**Paul** (*moving* DL *and kneeling to unroll his carpet and look at his purchases*) Money's all they seem to understand.

*The Servant enters up* R, *carrying a large cane chair which he places up* RC

**Lord Soper** Nonsense. They'd have recognized my authority eventually. (*Dropping in the chair, to the Servant's annoyance*) You! Get me a glass of iced tea.

*The Servant mutters savage Arabic gibberish and goes off up* R

**Paul** Most impressive, Soper.
**Lord Soper** Damn filthy place, Cairo. Can't wait to get out of it.

*Above, on the upper level, Nancy runs on in a bathing-suit, spreads out a towel and lies in the sun*

**Niven** (*setting up his camera up* R *and looking for subjects to photograph*) These things can't be rushed, Soper. Planning a proper expedition down the Nile takes time. There's the question of supplies, transport, all manner of paperwork.
**Lord Soper** Travel light, that's what I always say.
**Paul** (*sitting on the carpet down* L *and plucking at the instrument*) Where's Nancy got to?
**Niven** I think she's sunning herself on the roof. (*Waving to her*) Hallo, dear.
**Nancy** Hallo.
**Lord Soper** Hallo, darling.
**Nancy** Hallo.
**Paul** Hallo, dear.
**Nancy** Hallo.
**Niven** Is Mr Kemal at home, do you know, dear?
**Nancy** Yes, I think I heard him on to the telephone to that odd-job man of his—Mr Rouse—about our stores.
**Lord Soper** Well, I don't trust him. I'm sure he swindled us over those railway tickets.
**Niven** Of course he didn't.
**Nancy** Anybody can see that Mr Kemal is a gentleman.

**Lord Soper** (*sourly*) He's a gyp.
**Nancy** I didn't expect prejudice from *you*, Rodney.
**Lord Soper** (*surprised*) Why not?
**Niven** Ssh! Here he comes now.

*Eastern music*

*Kemal appears in the entrance C from behind the bead curtains R. He has changed into full Arab dress, burnous, head-dress, sword at his belt, etc. He holds out his arms to them*

**Kemal** Good morning, gentlemen. (*He claps his hands*)

*The Servant enters up R*

*Kemal speaks to the Servant in Arabic gibberish*

*The Servant replies, bows, and goes off through the bead curtains R*

*During the following, Kemal wanders in a little circle C, passing Lord Soper, Paul and Niven, and returning to his position up C*

**Kemal** I have ordered some iced tea. I trust you enjoyed your visit to the bazaar.
**Lord Soper** No, I did not. All those little urchins trying to sell their sisters. Do you know, one brat actually tried to sell me his little *brother*!
**Kemal** No doubt he spotted you were English.

*The Servant enters with tea on a silver tray*

Allow me. (*He takes two teas and passes them to Paul and Niven*)

*Rouse comes in from up C above the high level, R*

**Rouse** All right, all. (*To Kemal*) The stores are ready, sir.
**Nancy** Oh, jolly good. (*Rising*) I'll pop off and get ready, then.
**Niven** Just a moment, dear. Smile.

*Nancy poses. Niven's camera goes off with a flash of smoke*

*Nancy runs off L*

**Kemal** You can leave whenever you wish, gentlemen.
**Lord Soper** How about right now this minute?
**Niven** I agree. There's a good part of the day left. (*Making to go L*) Let's get our gear.
**Kemal** One moment.

*Niven pauses*

The Nile can be a dangerous river.

*Rouse nods and wanders down R during the following*

And then there is the desert beyond. You will need a guide—someone who knows the region well.
**Niven** Yes, I see what you mean.

## Act I, Scene 7

**Lord Soper** No doubt you have someone in mind, Kemal.
**Kemal** I think I can find you the ideal person. (*He claps his hands*)

*Mysterious Eastern music*

> *The Servant runs behind the bead curtain* R, *divests himself of the tray, then reappears* R *of the entrance* C, *up stage of the upper level.*
>
> *Ashayet, now beautifully dressed and looking glamorous and mysterious, enters* L *up stage of the upper level, as far up stage and as close to the cyclorama as possible before turning to face front and making the full walk from this position, down through the entrance, to up* C

*The music stops*

You will find none better. Her name is Ashayet.
**Paul** How do you do, Miss Ashayet?
**Niven** My pleasure, madam.
**Lord Soper** (*rising in disgust*) A woman! (*He moves behind his chair to up* RC)

*Kemal speaks to Ashayet in Arabic gibberish. Ashayet replies with a single word, and moves down* R

**Kemal** Good. You are in luck. She agrees. We will be ready to leave as soon as you wish.
**Niven** *We?*
**Kemal** Yes, I also am coming. I am curious to see what you discover.
**Niven** Oh, I'm sorry, can't permit that, Kemal, I'm afraid.
**Kemal** You have no choice, Professor. The supplies are mine, the boat is mine. It is only natural I should wish to share in the proceeds.
**Niven** But good heavens, Kemal, this is a *scientific* expedition!
**Kemal** Yes, they are usually the most profitable.
**Lord Soper** And if we refuse?
**Kemal** You will miss the flood season. That could delay you a year.
**Lord Soper** Got us over a barrel.
**Paul** Sounds fair enough to me, sir.
**Lord Soper** Who asked *you*, Conway? Button your lip.
**Niven** I suppose we'll have to agree, then. Goes against the grain, but yes—yes, we agree.
**Kemal** I thought you might, Professor. (*He moves down to Ashayet and they murmur in Arabic gibberish together*)
**Lord Soper** (*moving to Niven*) Don't trust that fellow. Never have done.
**Kemal** (*turning to them*) She says the dhow is moored close by. We should go aboard immediately.
**Paul** Dhow?
**Niven** Yes, the traditional Egyptian Nile River Boat, unchanged in design since the time of the Pharaohs.
**Lord Soper** Well, let's get aboard the blessed thing. Can't wait to shake the dust of this place off my boots.

*Nancy enters brightly from behind the bead curtain* L, *coming between Lord Soper and Niven to up* LC. *She is now wearing white jodphurs, white silk shirt, white topi*

**Nancy** Well, here I am, everybody—all ready for the fray.

*Nancy stops as she sees Ashayet. Flute and bells. Ashayet turns on her with almost a snarl, hissing in venomous Arabic gibberish. Nancy recoils to Lord Soper and Niven. Paul rises and joins her*

**Niven** What's the matter, Kemal?
**Kemal** I don't know. (*He asks Ashayet in Arabic gibberish*)
**Lord Soper** (*in a low voice*) Rum business this, Nancy—she seemed to recognize you.
**Paul** *Have* you seen her before?
**Nancy** I'm not sure. She seems familiar somehow—and yet . . . No—no—I've never seen her before.
**Kemal** We should proceed to the dhow. (*He moves* URC, *clapping his hands to the Servant and indicating he should clear the palm tree and chair*) Mr Rouse—see to the luggage.
**Rouse** (*tearing his eyes away from Ashayet*) Right, guv.

*Rouse goes off up* R

**Kemal** (*indicating they should follow him*) Please.

*Lord Soper, Niven, Paul go off up* R

*Mysterious Eastern music. Nancy goes more slowly. As she moves, Ashayet crosses below her, keeping her face turned to her, to* C

*Nancy runs off*

*Kemal comes quickly down to Ashayet and speaks in urgent, querying Arabic gibberish. Ashayet replies in dismissive, imperious Arabic gibberish*

*Ashayet goes off up* R. *Kemal follows her. The Servant, having cleared the palm tree, quickly takes the cane chair off* R *above the bead curtain*

*The music builds strongly*

## Scene 8

*Aboard the dhow. A bright moonlit night*

*The dhow glides on from up* R *pushed by two A.S.M.s Its main scenic feature is the large curved sail. The travellers are seated or standing on it in their various positions: Ashayet standing at the front, Niven seated behind her, studying his map, Paul and Kemal standing with the mast between them, leaning their backs against it, Paul to* L *playing the instrument, Kemal to* R, *Lord Soper seated with his feet stretched comfortably on the gunwale, cleaning his rifle, Nancy seated behind him, gazing about her, Rouse standing at rear working the rudder. Gentle River music continues from the last link, and con tinues under the dialogue. The timing of the following dialogue should be so organized that the Dhow has reached its final central position by Rouse's line "Two degrees to starboard, it is, sir"*

*Ashayet speaks Arabic gibberish*

**Niven** I think she wants you to turn a little to port, Kemal.
**Kemal** I know what she wants, Professor. Two degrees to starboard, Mr Rouse.
**Rouse** Two degrees to starboard, it is, sir. (*To the A.S.M.s*) Thanks, wacks.

*The A.S.M.s acknowledge his thanks, and go*

**Nancy** I say, Daddy, isn't the river beautiful by moonlight! Look at the *size* of it!
**Kemal** Yes—it is the flood season.
**Niven** The annual flood that has made the Nile so important since the dawn of history. It provides an irrigated area on either bank which would otherwise just be desert.
**Ashayet** (*pointing in front of them, almost chanting mysterious Arabic gibberish, ending with the one recognizable word*) . . . Karnak.
**Niven** By jove—yes—look—it's Karnak—the site of the ancient Egyptian city of Thebes. We're nearly there.

*Sombre music. Niven indicates up stage and all look*

On the East Bank, the city of the living. And on the West Bank . . .

*They all face down stage*

**Ashayet** The City of the Dead.
**Niven** (*in a hushed voice*) A whole Necropolis, devoted to the care of the dead and their preservation for the afterlife. It was from here that Inmutef-Amun was sent into the desert on his last journey, all those thousands of years ago.
**Paul** What are those ruins, Professor?
**Niven** Temples, mainly—to Amun-Ra—the extinct religion of the Sun God.
**Ashayet** No. Amun-Ra still lives. Each day, he rises anew. Each day, he lives again. All the gods live.

### SONG 4: Gods of Old

(*Speaking—almost in a whisper*)
    Nekhebet! Amun!
    Ishtar! Atum!
    Ernutet! Khnum!

    Isis! Osiris!
    Horus! Nephthys!

(*Singing*)   Mighty Ra!
    Mighty Ra!

> Gods of old
> All power over men
> Masters of all time and space
> Gods of old
> Rule over us again
> Shine benignly on my face
> Gods of glory
> Friends to all believers
> Shine your grace
> Upon my face
>
> Anubis! Heket!
> Sebek! Maet!
> Harakhti! Djet!
>
> Serket! Nekhen!
> Hathor! Mehen!
> Mighty Ra!
> Mighty Ra! ... Ah
>
> Gods of glory
> Friends to all believers
> Shine your grace
> Upon my face
> Shine your grace
> Upon my face

**Nancy** Oh look! What a big fish!

*Nancy puts her hand in the water. There is a loud crackle and a blue flash. She screams and jumps to her feet*

**Kemal** The giant electric catfish.
**Niven** Don't *do* that, dear—I'm trying to work out this map.
**Nancy** Cripes. It's straightened out my perm.
**Rouse** Suits you, miss.

*Nancy sits. Ashayet speaks venomous Arabic gibberish*

**Paul** (*in a low voice*) I don't think that woman likes you, my dear.
**Nancy** Most women don't, my dear.
**Lord Soper** And will you cut out that infernal twanging, Conway. It's getting on my wick.
**Paul** Philistine. I bought this in the Bazaar. Cost me three shillings.
**Lord Soper** Well, you were robbed.

*Ashayet points down L, speaking more gentle Arabic gibberish*

**Nancy** I say! What a pretty little antelope.

*They follow it with their eyes as it apparently runs from L to R down stage of the dhow*

## Act I, Scene 8

**Niven** It's a gazelle, my dear—anti-dorcas marsupialis.
**Paul** Sweet little thing, isn't it?

*Lord Soper shoots the animal. Ashayet screams venomous Arabic gibberish. Niven rises and goes to hold her and calm her*

**Nancy** Rodney!
**Niven** What the devil did you do that for, man?
**Lord Soper** Just testing my sights.

*Ashayet wails*

**Kemal** You are a fool, my lord. She says the Gazelle is sacred to the Sun God.
**Lord Soper** Rubbish.
**Rouse** Quite apart from shooting a dear little deer, just for the fun of it.
**Lord Soper** It wasn't that much fun, Rouse. It was standing still.
**Paul** Ssh!
**Niven** What is it?
**Paul** I think I can hear something.

*All strain to hear*

Hear that? Like a sort of whispering?
**Lord Soper** (*rising, rifle ready, peering off* R) It's coming from behind us, I think!
**Rouse** You're right, sir.
**Lord Soper** Can't see a damned thing!
**Kemal** (*forcing himself past Paul and pointing* L) That's because it's coming from in front of us!
**Rouse** *You're* right, sir.
**Kemal** It's a cataract!

*There is an immediate loud, deafening, roar of white water*

**Niven** Quick, Kemal—take us into the bank!
**Kemal** Starboard, Rouse! Starboard!
**Rouse** (*heaving at the rudder*) Starboard, it is, sir!
**Lord Soper** Into the bank, man! Get me into the bank!

*There is a loud crash. The A.S.M.s off* R *jerk ropes attached to the rear of the dhow. All are thrown forward by the apparent impact*

**Niven** We've struck a rock!
**Paul** (*looking over the side*) We're holed!
**Nancy** (*screaming and climbing on to her seat*) Ah! There's water coming in!
**Rouse** Bail for your lives!

*Rouse, Niven and Paul start bailing*

**Kemal** Don't worry! The rock is holding her steady and preventing the boat from turning turtle and drowning us!

*They pause in their bailing*

**Lord Soper** Then we're safe!
**Kemal** Until the flood level rises.
**Niven** Then what happens?
**Kemal** The boat turns turtle and we drown.

*Rouse, Niven and Paul yell and bail harder*

**Lord Soper** You blithering incompetent idiot, Kemal! Trust a gyppy to gyp you!
**Kemal** (*clapping his hands to his dagger*) You will not insult me again and live, you fat English homosexual pig!
**Lord Soper** What do you mean, fat?

*Ashayet murmurs Arabic gibberish, as if casting a spell, and waves a hand to down* R. *All stop what they are doing and peer over the downstage side*

**Paul** Look—the stern's swinging into the bank. We can jump ashore.
**Niven** Quickly, then!

*Paul begins to help Nancy out of the boat*

**Kemal** Mr Rouse! Take the painter!
**Rouse** Right, sir!

*Rouse jumps ashore and runs across* L, *reaches for the painter at the prow and hangs on to it for dear life. Niven clambers out to help him. Nancy moves down* R. *Paul turns to help Ashayet out. Lord Soper jumps ashore*

Give us a hand here, Soper!
**Lord Soper** *Lord Soper* to you, Rouse, you little scouse! (*Nevertheless, he hurries* L, *puts down his rifle and helps hang on to the painter*)
**Kemal** Hold her, Rouse! Hold her!

*Paul hurries across* L *to help*

**Rouse** I can't hold her much longer, sir!
**Nancy** Jump, Mr Kemal! Jump!
**Kemal** No—we need these supplies!
**Rouse** You'll have to, sir! She's going!

*All collapse, and the dhow glides off back the way it came,* R. *Kemal jumps ashore just in time.*

**Lord Soper** You idiot, Rouse!
**Niven** We'll have to catch up with her downstream!
**Rouse** Leave it to me, sir—*I'll* do it!

*Rouse goes off* R, *careful to stay on "dry land" and not walk in what is still "the river"*

**Lord Soper** Too late, man—come back—she's going under!

*Descending music*

**Nancy** There she goes now.

## Act I, Scene 8

*All look off* R. *The descending music finishes. There is a silence*

Well, Daddy? Now what?
**Lord Soper** Yes, Niven—we're stranded here—unless another boat comes along.
**Paul** Where are we anyway?
**Niven** Haven't the foggiest, I'm afraid.
**Ashayet** (*in Arabic gibberish, indicating*) The Belly of Stones.
**Niven** By jove, yes, she's right, look! *It is* the Belly of Stones!
**Nancy** What's that, Daddy?
**Niven** It's a desolate rocky region between Karnak and Aswan. But I think—yes—we've alighted exactly where the map says!
**Paul** Odd, really.
**Lord Soper** Yes—funny sort of coincidence.

*All look at Ashayet and Kemal. Flute and bells music*

**Kemal** Well then, it seems we have a choice. Either we turn back and follow the river where there is water—or we . . .?
**Ashayet** Go on.
**Kemal** Which is it to be?
**Niven** Well, I'm afraid with our supplies at the bottom of the Nile, there is no alternative but to abandon the expedition—temporarily, of course.
**Lord Soper** Oh, drat!

*Sad music. They squat, crouch, generally look depressed. A long pause*

**Rouse** (*off*) Hey! Hey!

*Rouse runs on, carrying bundles, packs, a folding chair*

Look what I managed to save! The tent and some of the packs!

*General congratulations. All converge on Rouse and clap him on the back, except Nancy, Ashayet and Kemal*

**Niven** That puts a different complexion on things! We go on! Share out the loads and follow me! (*He makes his way off down* L)
**Lord Soper** (*rushing across* L *and grabbing up his rifle*) No, let me go first—I'm a born leader!

*Paul, Niven and Lord Soper go off down* L

**Nancy** (*running to Rouse*) Well done, Mr Rouse!

*Nancy kisses Rouse and follows the others off*

*Mysterious eastern music. Ashayet looks at Kemal*

*Kemal goes off down* L

*Ashayet goes to Rouse, who is busy arranging the packs. She puts a finger under his chin and lifts him*

**Ashayet** Come with me and I will make you my slave.

*Ashayet goes off down* L

*Rouse gazes off after her in rapture*

**Rouse** Her *slave*! I'm going to be her *slave*! (*Picking up the packs*) I'm going up in the world. I'm going to be her slave.

*Rouse goes off down* L

## Scene 9

*Ruins in the Desert*

*There is an immediate loud howl of wind, and dim amber lighting*

*Lord Soper, Niven, Paul, Kemal, Nancy and Ashayet come on from up stage of the high level* R. *All cover their faces from the sandstorm*

**Lord Soper** (*shouting*) Shouldn't we rest, Professor? We can't see where we're going in this sandstorm!
**Niven** (*shouting*) I'm looking for some shelter!
**Lord Soper** (*coming through* C *entrance up* LC *and indicating the ruined temple* L) What are these?
**Niven** (*joining him*) By jove, yes—look—ruins!
**Lord Soper** Let's get in the lee of these walls! In the lee of the walls, everybody!

*Lord Soper ushers Niven down* L, *followed by Kemal, who is protecting Ashayet from the storm with the folds of his burnous. Paul, handkerchief over face is holding on to Nancy, but she breaks down* R

**Paul** I say, Nancy, don't go wandering off—if we get separated in this thing, we're doomed.
**Nancy** I'll be all right over here.
**Lord Soper** (*shouting over*) What are you playing at, Conway? Bring Nancy over here!
**Paul** (*staggering across* L) I'm trying to, you miserable duffer! She prefers to be on her own!

*By now, they are settling down to ride out the sandstorm in the shelter of the ruins, down* L

*Rouse staggers in to join them, still carrying packs, etc., which he dumps just beside and partially behind the profile*

*Ashayet and Kemal squat* C *of the group, Paul and Niven to the* R, *Lord Soper to the* L, *Rouse crouches above them, up stage*

**Rouse** How long before this storm blows itself out, Mr Kemal?
**Kemal** It is the will of Allah.
**Ashayet** No. It is the will of Amun-Ra. It will be soon.
**Niven** Soon? Don't know about that, my dear—these things usually blow for days.
**Ashayet** No. It will be soon. You will see.

## Act I, Scene 9

*The roar of the wind fades away to a whisper and to silence. The scene perceptibly brightens*

**Lord Soper** I say! (*Staring at Ashayet*) How extraordinary!

*All stare at her*

**Nancy** I say, Daddy, now the sandstorm's passed, you can really see these ruins properly.

**Niven** (*rising and joining her*) Yes, by jove—late period—Thirtieth Dynasty, by the look of it. You can see the Greek and Persian influence.

**Paul** Cleopatra, what?

**Ashayet** (*in contempt*) Cleopatra? That little nobody!

*Music, as Ashayet rises*

It is only fitting she killed herself with the sacred cobra.

**Lord Soper** I thought it was an asp.

**Ashayet** No, a cobra.

**Niven** You seem to know an awful lot about those times, Ashayet.

**Ashayet** (*moving* C) Cleopatra? That is not so long ago. (*Crossing up to the C entrance, her hands high as if worshipping the old temple*) The glory that was Egypt vanished long before.

*Ashayet goes off* L

**Lord Soper** I could have sworn it was an asp.

**Niven** Yes, well, its nearly dark and this seems as good a spot as any. (*Moving to the gear*) I suggest we pitch the tent and make camp.

**Paul** (*rising*) Here here. My feet are killing me. And I need my dinner.

**Niven** We'll have to be careful, though, Conway—we've very little left in the way of rations.

**Paul** (*putting his arm round Nancy*) At least we can serve it properly.

**Nancy** I agree.

*During the above, Rouse opens up the folding chair and sets it down* R

*Rouse exits up* R

**Paul** (*romantically*) After all—desert sky—romantic surroundings—

*Lord Soper crosses in front of Paul, totally uninterested in romantic surroundings, and sits in the chair*

—the tumbled ruins of history. All we need is a little light music.

*Rouse pushes on the piano up* R

**Lord Soper** Oh, God.

**Paul** (*moving to the piano*) Rouse! You're a gem! (*He tosses his coat on the piano, makes sure his sleeves are firmly rolled up and prepares to play*) Ladies and gentlemen, I would like you to imagine this is a four-thousand-year-old piano. (*He plays an arpeggio*) It *is* a four-thousand-year-old piano.

**Lord Soper** (*impatiently rising and moving further down* R) Come on, everybody—let's make camp!

*Paul sings. During the song, they make camp. Niven and Rouse unfold the card table and three little wooden camping stools from the pile of gear. Niven then lays the table with paper plates, cups, apples and biscuits. Rouse then concentrates on opening a bottle of champagne and seeing that everybody gets a cupful. Nancy carries food and champagne across to the pianist at some point, and also goes off into the desert to find a nice little palm or cactus to put on the table in lieu of flowers. Kemal sets up the tent, which is stretched across the* C *entrance, the sides sloping diagonally to down stage of this and stretched on weights. The flaps for entering the tent are then* R *and* L. *This cannot be detailed in the song, and is best left fairly free. The important thing is that by the end of the song, the camp is set up, Lord Soper is stretched out comfortably in his chair, sipping champagne. Niven is seated at the table* L, *Kemal seated at the table* R, *Nancy seated at the table, down* C. *Rouse standing over them, serving. Lord Soper takes no part in the building of the camp. After adjusting his dress and hair, he sits again at the chair*

### SONG 5: Life is Full of Mysteries

**Paul**     History is all around us
　　　　　　Its mystery will always last
　　　　　　Everything we take for granted
　　　　　　Is just a product of the past

　　　　　　When the caveman first invented the wheel
　　　　　　He turned to Missis Caveman and said, I feel
　　　　　　That when I've perfected my ideal
　　　　　　We'll be riding high
　　　　　　In the sky

　　　　　　And the world won't be the same any more
　　　　　　There's a whole new game for us to explore
　　　　　　That'll change the ways that we went before
　　　　　　Don't know how or why. All I know is—

**Paul**　　⎫ Life is full of mysteries
**Nancy**　⎬ And history's taught this to me
　　　　　　That if life has no mystery
　　　　　　Then what is life at all?

**Rouse**　　Yeah yeah yeah!
**Paul and**
**Nancy**　 ⎬ If life has no mystery
**Rouse**　　Then what is life at all?
**Niven**　　When the apple fell on Newton's head
　　　　　　He jumped up, by jove, and he said
　　　　　　Feathers can fall as fast as lead
　　　　　　Don't know why but they do
**Nancy** (*returning with the little palm*)
　　　　　　Ticketyboo!
　　　　　　When Archimedes leapt out of the bath

## Act I, Scene 9

                And ran stark naked down his garden path
                His theory exposed in spite of the draught
                He was heard to shriek—

*Rouse pops the champagne cork*

**Lord Soper**   Eureka!

**All**            The world won't be the same any more
                You close one chapter, open the door
                To a whole new set of puzzles galore
                Don't ask me why but it's true

**Paul**           All I know is . . .

**All**            Life is full of mysteries
                And history's taught this to me
                That if life has no mystery
                Then what is life at all?

**Rouse**         Yeah yeah yeah!

**All**            If life has no mystery
                Then what is life at all?

**Paul**           History is ever growing
                You learn a little more each day
                And there will always be some knowing
                Genius who'll rise and say . . .

**Rouse**         Two three four!

**All**            The world won't be the same any more
                It's a basic scientific law
                It's a fact, my friends, that you can't ignore
                Don't ask me why but it's true
                All I know is . . .

                Life is full of mysteries
                And history's taught this to me
                That if life has no mystery
                Then what is life at all?

**Rouse**         Yeah yeah yeah!

**All**            If life has no mystery
                Then what is life at all?
                Oh yeah!

*Paul pushes the piano off up R and joins the group at the table. The Band continues with party music. There is general chatter from everybody*

   *After a while, the Taureg comes on slowly up* R, *his lower face masked, a rifle in the crook of his arm*

*The Band fades away. The chatter also gradually fades until there is silence. Niven sees the Taureg last of all*

**Niven** (*rising*) Good Lord, it's a Taureg!

*Lord Soper knocks his chair over and hastily moves* L. *Kemal and Nancy rise*

**Paul** What does he want? Our water?
**Nancy** (*going to the Taureg*) Oh yes. (*Offering him her glass of champagne*) Water? *Aqua minerale?*

*The Taureg looks her up and down*

**Niven** I don't think it's quite that simple, my dear.

*The Taureg gives Nancy's behind a good feel, and she shrieks. He calls across to Niven in Arabic gibberish, working his thumb and forefinger*

**Lord Soper** What did he say?
**Niven** (*repeating the Taureg's Arabic gibberish exactly*) Which, roughly translated, means . . .
**Kemal** How much for the little white dish?
**Niven** That's it.
**Nancy** You mean he wants to buy me? (*Running back to the group*)
**Paul**  ⎫
**Lord Soper** ⎬ My fiancée? { (*Speaking together*)
**Paul** You filthy beggar!

*Paul puts up fists but Rouse drags him back. Lord Soper goes to the Taureg, very authoritatively*

**Lord Soper** Now look here, my name's Lord Soper, and I'm a member of His Britannic Majesty's aristocracy . . .

*The Taureg hits Lord Soper in the stomach with his rifle. Lord Soper collapses. The Taureg speaks much more peremptory Arabic gibberish*

**Niven** I'm afraid that was a little quick for me, Kemal. What did he say?
**Kemal** He says if we don't sell her to him, he will stake us out in the desert for the vultures to peck out our eyes.
**Niven** Leave this to me. Rouse—hand me that sack of glass beads and tin kazoos I brought for just such an emergency.

*The Taureg speaks contemptuous Arabic gibberish, spitting. Nancy, Paul, Rouse and Niven ask Kemal—all at the same time, but in their own individual ways, not a chorus—what the Taureg has just said*

**Kemal** He says, keep your decadent western trash. He only wants to buy the bint.
**Nancy** Bint?
**Niven** Ah yes, well, in that case . . . (*He launches himself into long Arabic gibberish*)

*Brief pause*

**Lord Soper** ⎫
**Nancy** ⎬ (*to Kemal*) What did *he* say? { (*Speaking together*)
**Paul** ⎭
**Kemal** He said he can have you in exchange for one camel.

**Nancy** Daddy!
**Niven** Oh, don't worry, my dear—no Arab would part with a camel in exchange for a mere woman.

*The Taureg snaps his fingers and a Camel's head appears up* R

Ah . . . !

*The Taureg speaks cheerful gibberish as he gives the reins to Niven, goes to Nancy, and begins to drag her off* R. *Lord Soper, recovering, grabs his rifle and comes down* C

**Lord Soper** I'm not standing for this! Let her go, you damned lecherous golliwog! (*He aims the rifle*)

*The Taureg turns and fires quickly, knocking the rifle from Lord Soper's hands. He drops to his knees, wringing his hands in pain. Fast music, dramatic. The Taureg reloads and aims, cursing them in Arabic gibberish. Nancy screams*

**Kemal** Look out! He'll kill us all!

*The music suddenly changes: Eastern, mysterious*

*Ashayet comes on down* L. *The Taureg sees her and immediately cowers, murmuring awed Arabic gibberish: as she crosses towards him he slowly backs off until he is gone*

*There is a silence*

**Niven** (*moving to Ashayet*) Why was he frightened of you, Ashayet?
**Ashayet** Who can say? They are only children.
**Niven** Tauregs? They're one of the most bloodthirsty tribes in the world.
**Paul** (*holding out his hands to Nancy*) It's all right, Nancy, dear—we wouldn't have let him touch you.
**Nancy** (*going to Paul*) No, I know you wouldn't Paul—Rodney—Mr Kemal . . .
**Niven** Well—after all this excitement, I certainly don't feel like eating. (*Picking up Lord Soper's chair*) I suggest we get an early night. Rouse— help me clear up, will you?
**Rouse** Right you are, sir.

*During the following, Rouse and Niven clear away the table, stools, etc. Niven also sorts out a couple of blankets*

**Paul** I take it the ladies share the tent.
**Niven** Of course.
**Nancy** (*looking uneasily at Ashayet*) Actually, Daddy, no offence, but I've always been a Day Girl.
**Ashayet** Is all right. I sleep out here.

*Ashayet glides off into the desert up* R

**Niven** Good, that's settled then. (*He drops the blankets*) Good-night, dear.
**Nancy** Good-night, Daddy. (*She kisses Niven*)

*Niven goes off down* L

Good-night, Paul. (*She kisses Paul*)
**Paul** Good-night, dear.
**Nancy** Good-night, Rodney. (*She kisses Lord Soper*)
**Lord Soper** Good-night, darling.
**Nancy** Good-night, Mr Rouse. (*She kisses Rouse*)
**Rouse** Good-night, miss.

*Rouse goes off up* L

**Nancy** Good-night, Mr— (*she goes to kiss Kemal, then holds out her hand*) —Kemal.
**Kemal** Good-night, Miss Niven. Pleasant dreams.
**Nancy** Oh, I'm sure they will be. Good night.

*Nancy goes into the tent from* L. *Paul and Lord Soper glare at Kemal and, having picked up their blankets earlier, prepare to bed down* R. *Kemal starts to go off down* L. *A light comes on in the tent. Sultry saxophone music. Kemal pauses, turns and looks. Lord Soper and Paul stop what they are doing and look. On the walls of the tent is a perfect silhouette of Nancy getting undressed. After a moment, Paul sees Kemal looking and nudges Lord Soper. Lord Soper goes to Kemal*

**Lord Soper** You, sir, are not a gentleman!
**Kemal** I never said I was. Good-night.

*Kemal goes off down* L

*Lord Soper turns and looks at Nancy's silhouette*

**Lord Soper** Women just aren't safe with a certain sort of chap. I mean, apart from anything else, the fellow's a dago. It's just not on.
**Paul** (*looking at the silhouette*) You'd think she'd understand. She's been well brought up. She goes to the same hairdresser as my mother.

*Brief pause*

**Lord Soper**  
**Paul** } Actually, I think I'll ... { (*Speaking together*)
**Lord Soper** Sorry. You were saying?
**Paul** I was saying I think I'll sleep out here.
**Lord Soper** Yes, me too. Me too.

*They tear their eyes away from Nancy*

Well, come on, man!

*They get their blankets and curl up in them down* R. *The music stops. Nancy puts on a dressing gown and brushes her hair. A hissing noise is heard, then the silhouette of a Giant Cobra is seen, gliding into the tent behind her. Nancy leans forward to pick up something. As she does so, it strikes at the back of ner neck and misses. She resumes brushing her hair. It draws back to strike. She drops the brush, bends to pick it up. The Cobra strikes again and misses again*

*Kemal comes on down* L. *He has divested himself of his head-dress and his outer robes*

**Kemal** Excuse me, gentlemen, I wonder if I could borrow a bar of . . .

*Kemal sees the Cobra, curses in Arabic gibberish and rushes into the tent,* L. *Nancy, rushes out of the tent,* R, *and goes down to Lord Soper and Paul, who rise and protect her. In silhouette, we see Kemal's fight to the death with the Giant Cobra, gripping its neck, ducking its strikes, falling over, reversing, the coils of its body around his neck. Music throughout. Eventually, he is able to draw his knife and stab it. The head and body falls back limp in his hands. The music stops. Kemal comes out from the tent,* L, *and throws the body of the Cobra on the ground* C

It is dead.

*They crowd about it, still nervous of it*

**Lord Soper** It's the biggest cobra I've ever seen.
**Paul** I wonder how it got into her tent.

*Ashayet appears up* R

**Ashayet** It smelt her.

*All jump. Music: mysterious, Eastern*

**Nancy** Pardon?
**Ashayet** (*moving to the snake and kneeling beside it*) It smelt the warmth. (*Accusingly, to Kemal*) You should not have killed him. (*She picks it up, cradling it to her face and neck lovingly*)
**Nancy** Look here, it was either the snake or me!
**Ashayet** That is so.

*Ashayet glides off down* L

**Nancy** Well—thank you once again, Mr Kemal.
**Lord Soper** Yes, well done, old boy.
**Paul** Splendid show.
**Nancy** Good-night.

*Nancy goes into the tent again. The others half move towards it, but the light goes out*

**Lord Soper** Oh.
**Kemal** Well, gentlemen, I suggest we take a look around—just in case, you understand.
**Lord Soper** I agree.

*They all go off up* R

*The music rises to a climax, and the Lights fade to a Black-out*

## Scene 10

*In the Desert Above the Tomb*

*Voices are heard in the Black-out*

**Lord Soper** (*off*) Look here, Professor, are you sure you know where you're going?
**Niven** (*off*) Of course. I've got the map, haven't I?
**Lord Soper** (*off*) If it's reliable.

*Lord Soper comes on up* R

*The Lights come up, very hot and bright—sweltering heat in the middle of the desert. Everyone is hot, exhausted and thirsty*

What are you going to use for landmarks? There's nothing out here but a lot of sand. (*He appears to step in something*) Bloody camels! (*Scraping it off with the butt of his rifle*) How do you map a lot of sand, man?

*Niven comes on up* R *and crosses* L

**Niven** There are wadis and ridges and depressions—enough to know where one's going—so stop worrying, Soper.
**Lord Soper** I'm not worried. I just want to get there.

*Paul staggers on up* R. *He has a pack on his back, his sleeves rolled up and wears his old cricket cap. He is exhausted*

**Paul** How much further, Professor?
**Niven** Not far now.
**Paul** (*dropping to his knees*) I don't think I can go on much longer.
**Niven** (*moving to Paul*) Nonsense, my boy—if *I* can do it, *you* can do it. Here, have a drop of water. (*He offers Paul his canteen*)

*Paul grabs it desperately and gulps the water, but Niven has to be firm with him*

Not too much, my boy.
**Paul** It's this damned heat.
**Lord Soper** Yes. Nearly as bad as the Gobi. Lost three bearers there once. Damn frightful place. It was them or me, I'm afraid.
**Paul** You mean you *abandoned* them?
**Lord Soper** Good Lord, no. Ate them. One has to do that sort of thing occasionally, you know.

*Ashayet comes on up* R, *followed by the exhausted Rouse, who carries a pack, and has a red knotted handkerchief over his head*

**Paul** Well, Margate's my limit in future.
**Ashayet** Why do we stop?
**Niven** Just checking. Here, have a drink. (*He offers her the canteen*)
**Ashayet** (*waving it away contemptuously*) Pah!

## Act I, Scene 10

**Rouse** I must say you look remarkably cool, madam. How do you do it?
**Ashayet** One can get used to anything if there is sufficient time.
**Lord Soper** Rouse, where's Nancy?
**Rouse** I've no idea, sir.

*Kemal comes on up R*

Oh, here's Mr Kemal. Have you seen our Miss Nancy, sir?
**Kemal** She dropped behind. She has some sand in her shoe. Quite a lot. (*To Niven and Paul*) I shouldn't sit there if I were you, gentlemen.
**Paul** Why?
**Kemal** Scorpions.

*They yell, jump up, brush at their clothes*

**Niven** Never a dull moment, eh, Soper?

*Nancy comes on up R carrying shoes in her hand and comes slowly down to them.*

**Kemal** Miss Niven—let me assist you. (*Taking her arm*) You don't look well.
**Nancy** (*in a dead voice*) I'm all right.
**Ashayet** (*impatiently*) I ask again—why do we *stop*?
**Niven** (*admitting it, reluctantly*) I'm not sure. I don't seem to be able to see the next landmark.
**Lord Soper** Do you mean we're lost!
**Niven** Oh no, no, we're not lost. We should be able to find our way back to the river again—with any luck. We're not lost.
**Ashayet** (*furiously*) Who cares about the river? Where is the tomb of Inmutef-Amun?
**Niven** Well, we ought to be right on top of it, but as you can see for yourself there's nothing here but sand and rock.
**Nancy** No.

*Flute and bells music is heard*

He's here.
**Paul** What are you talking about, Nancy?
**Nancy** Inmutef-Amun. He's here. (*She walks slowly up C, as if sleep-walking*)
**Lord Soper** But . . .
**Ashayet** Sssh!

*Nancy stops on the trap, turns and faces front*

**Nancy** Here.

*All look at her feet*

**Paul** There's nothing there, darling. It's just sand and rock.

*Flute and bells. Nancy seems to wake up, and staggers dizzily down R*

**Nancy** I'm sorry—what was I saying? I came over all dizzy.

**Paul** It's all right—it's just the heat.
**Niven** (*on his knees, excitedly*) No, by jove! She's right! Look here!

*All hurry to join him*

**Nancy** Hairyglyphics.
**Niven** Hieroglyphs! It's a tomb, by the look of things. Let's see if I can translate. (*He polishes his magnifying glass and holds it up to see if it is clean. The sun neatly burns a hole in his eye, and he reacts*)
**Rouse** That could have been nasty, sir.

*Music as Niven translates, Lord Soper brushes away the "sand" from the characters. Ashayet faces front, down* L, *her lips forming the words until, eventually, she takes over from Niven*

**Niven** To Amun-Ra, Lord of the Thrones of the Two Lands, King of Eternity, Lord of Everlastingness, Ruler, Lord of the Two Great Plumes—
**Ashayet** —Sole One, Primordial, Eldest, Creator of Gods and men—

*They rise, staring at her*

—protect thy Servant, thy only servant—Inmutef-Amun!

*Ashayet turns, holding out her hands in supplication to the grave. The music stops*

**Paul** I thought you said the grave was unmarked.
**Niven** So they reported back. But Inmutef-Amun was a powerful man and served a powerful god.
**Lord Soper** Give me that spade, Rouse! Step back, everybody!

*Lord Soper stands on the trap and digs furiously. Ragtime music. The trap goes slowly down with him on it until he is out of sight. The music stops. There is the clang of a spade, and a yell from Lord Soper*

**Niven** What have you found?
**Lord Soper** (*his head appearing*) Solid rock.
**Ashayet** No. Look more closely. The mortar will have been carved to look like rock.
**Niven** Out of the way, Soper! (*He jumps down*) By jove, she's right, it crumbles if you hit it!
**Lord Soper** Rouse—my rifle!
**Rouse** Right, sir! (*He fetches it for him*)
**Paul** What can you see beyond, sir?
**Niven** (*his head appearing*) A tunnel! There's a tunnel in the rock!
**Lord Soper** (*taking the rifle*) There's more to this than meets the eye!

*Lord Soper and Niven vanish as Paul climbs in*

**Nancy** Do stop poking at it, Rodney! We've found the entrance. Can't we go home now?
**Paul** (*in the trap*) After we've come all this way? Come along, Nancy—there's nothing to be frightened of.

Act I, Scene 10   47

*Paul helps Nancy down*

**Rouse** I'll give you a hand, miss.

*Rouse jumps down. Music, mysterious, Eastern. Kemal lifts Ashayet and lowers her slowly, gracefully into the trap. He jumps down himself, looks around, vanishes. The music rises to a climax. The Lights fade to a Black-out*

SCENE 11

*The Tomb of Inmutef-Amun*

*The music continues, more sombre. Voices are heard off, down* L *as soon as the sarcophagus is in position*

**Lord Soper** (*off*) Can't see a damned thing!
**Niven** (*off*) We're in the outer chamber—but look!—any further entry is blocked by this huge stone!
**Ashayet** (*off*) There will be a counter-balance and a spring. Leave it to me.

*There is a loud grating of stone, and a shaft of light, very low on the floor shoots across* R *from down* L

**Lord Soper** (*off*) By jove, I think I can see something! Give me a push!

*Lord Soper climbs in down* L, *as if through very low tunnel, and crosses* R. *All entrances and exits in the tomb contain this same mime. He is followed by Niven who moves* C, *then Paul and Nancy*

**Niven** Good Lord! Look at this! It's been undisturbed for three and a half thousand years! (*Peering into the auditorium*) I suppose these must be the bones of his retainers.
**Paul** (*turning and seeing the sarcophagus*) Gosh, look at this!

*Paul moves* L *of the sarcophagus, Niven, Lord Soper to its* R. *Nancy goes down* R, *away from it. Rouse helps Ashayet into the tomb*

**Lord Soper** Rouse! My rifle!

*He throws it over to Rouse, who leaves it leaning against wall* L

**Niven** This is the culmination of my life's work!
**Lord Soper** Let's get the lid off. I'm dying to see what the blighter looks like.

*They struggle with the huge lid, Niven and Lord Soper* R, *Paul and Rouse* L

**Rouse** Up your end, Soper!
**Lord Soper** No, man—up yours, up yours!

*They continue instructions as they finally heave the lid off the tomb and lean it upright against the wall panel* L. *The huge figure of the Mummy is now revealed in the tomb. Music throughout, rising to a climax. They collect around him, Lord Soper to the* R *of the sarcophagus, Niven and Paul above it, Rouse* L *of the sarcophagus. During the following, Ashayet pushes Rouse out of the way and goes slowly round and above the sarcophagus, peering down at the face of the Mummy*

**Niven** Good Lord, look at the size of him! And in a state of almost perfect preservation!
**Paul** We could have done with him against the All Blacks.
**Lord Soper** This has been a bad trip for your inane comments, Conway. Keep them for the Playing Fields of Plaistow.

*They become aware of Ashayet's movement and all break away down R, uneasy and puzzled*

**Ashayet** Rouse.

*She holds up a leg, and Rouse helps her climb up on to the sarcophagus where she can peer down into the face of her lost love. The others do not know what's going on, but do not like the look of it at all*

**Lord Soper** Rouse.

*He indicates that Rouse should join them. They form a little whispering huddled group, R*

What do we do now, Professor?
**Niven** Only one thing we *can* do—get our breaths back, seal up the entrance again, and go back to Cairo for some equipment and to break the good news.
**Ashayet** No.

*Minor chords*

No-one must know. No-one *will* know.
**Lord Soper** What is she whittering on about?
**Ashayet** (*pointing to Nancy*) Ask *her*. *She* knows.
**Paul** What's she talking about, Nancy?
**Nancy** I don't know. At least, I don't *think* I do . . .
**Ashayet** You men of Science! You are all alike! You think you know all the secrets of life and death! But you know nothing! These secrets were known centuries before there *was* a word called Science! . . .
**Lord Soper** She's potty.
**Niven** Yes, I think a small, judicious retreat—just in case, you understand . . .
**Lord Soper** Right, everybody—follow me. (*He goes to lead them across* L)
**Ashayet** Kemal!

*Kemal appears from the tomb entrance, revolver pointed at them*

*All react and back down R*

**Kemal** I am sorry, everybody, but nobody is leaving here.
**Lord Soper** What's the meaning of this?
**Ashayet** Just do as he says! Unless you wish to go the way of all the others who have stood between me and my heart's desire!
**Nancy** And I thought you were ace! You—you—rotter, Kemal!

## Act I, Scene 11

**Ashayet** Kemal is my creature, and will be rewarded as I have promised him—with Eternal Life.
**Niven** What utter bosh!
**Ashayet** You think so, Professor? Then how old am I! Look deep into my eyes and tell me—how old am I?
**Niven** Well, I don't really like to say.
**Ashayet** (*to Paul*) You, then?
**Paul** Not really pukka—
**Lord Soper** —discussing a lady's age.
**Ashayet** (*to Nancy*) You, then.
**Nancy** Yes. I see it all now. You were there. All those thousands of years ago. She was there.
**Paul** You're joking, Nancy.
**Ashayet** No. Once one has bathed in the River of Life, one cannot die. Unlike *you*—(*spitting at Nancy*)—you pale reincarnation of a slave girl!

*Nancy falls to her knees*

> I killed you once and I will kill you again! I was banished and my lover bound and buried, both of us unable to die, but now I have found him again! (*To the Mummy*) Oh my lover, how long have I searched for thee! They hid thee well, but I knew that one day I would find thee again! And now—the Spell of Awakening!

*Music. Ashayet holds up her arms*

> Inmutef-Amun! Thy lover, Ashayet, calls to thee across the great years! Thou hast slept long, my beloved, but now thy sleep is over! Rise up! Kill the defilers of thy temple! Rejoin thy beloved! I command thee in the name of Mighty Ra! Rise up! Rise!

*The music rises to a climax and stops. Pause*

**Paul** I think he's overslept.
**Lord Soper** Barmy. Quite barmy.
**Kemal** (*furiously*) Be quiet! (*To Ashayet*) Try again!
**Ashayet** Come, my beloved! Come! We shall make thee young again! We shall bathe together in the River of Life! We shall drink the blood of the virgin! We shall rule again! Come, Inmutef-Amun! Thy lover, Ashayet, calls to thee!

*The music rises to a climax again and stops. Again, nothing happens, but this time Ashayet sways a little, looks faint and old, and begins to climb down off the sarcophagus*

**Paul** She's lost her marbles.
**Rouse** (*calling across to Kemal*) Is she all right, sir?
**Kemal** Be silent! (*To Ashayet*) What is wrong?
**Ashayet** It has been too many years. I must go back to Karnak for a stronger spell.
**Kemal** (*indicating the others*) And these?
**Ashayet** Let them die here . . .

*Cries of indignation from the others, as Ashayet goes down L to the exit*

They can do him no harm.
**Lord Soper** No—wait!
**Paul** At least let the lady go, Ashayet!
**Ashayet** She, least of all.

*Ashayet crouches and crawls off down L*

**Kemal** Rouse. (*As Rouse hesitates, he waves with the pistol*) Mr Rouse!

*Rouse moves C, and pauses, indicating the others*

**Rouse** What about *them*, sir?
**Kemal** (*threatening him with the pistol*) Would you like to stay with them?

*Rouse shrugs at them and goes off quickly, down L*

**Paul** Rouse!
**Lord Soper** You little louse!
**Kemal** Forgive me, Miss Niven.

*Kemal crouches and backs off, down L*

**Ashayet** (*off*) Release the stone!

*The grating of the stone is heard. Lord Soper and Paul rush across down L and push at it, off, but they obviously fail. The stone stops with a crash, the light pouring in from here is cut off*

**Lord Soper** We'll never shift that.

*Paul throws his pack in a corner and sits dejectedly against the sarcophagus*

What do you make of this tale, Professor?
**Niven** The ravings of a lunatic—what else?
**Lord Soper** I'm not so sure. (*Looking around*) It's a bit stuffy in here. How long before the air runs out?
**Niven** Half an hour at the most, I'm afraid.
**Lord Soper** Oh, blast.

*They are all very dejected*

**Nancy** Well—at least we're together. It's good to be with chums at a time like this.
**Niven** Quite.
**Paul** I agree, darling.
**Lord Soper** Yes. Got a point, old girl. And at least, he'll have some company soon . . .

*Lord Soper pats the sarcophagus familiarly. Unseen, behind them, one of the Mummy's hands jerks up. During the following, it begins to sit up very slowly, it's heavy breathing heard. Lord Soper holds out his hand to Paul*

Put it there, old chap.
**Paul** (*suspiciously*) What for? Indian wrestling?

Act I, Scene 11

**Lord Soper** No, want to make amends. Been dashed rude to you occasionally. She's yours.

**Paul** You're very magnanimous, now I can't have her. However . . .

*Paul and Lord Soper shake hands*

**Nancy** Well done, Rodney, I knew . . .

*By now, the Mummy is fully up and Nancy sees him*

Rodney!

*Nancy screams and runs around and up* R. *Niven, Paul and Lord Soper react away down* R. *The Mummy makes for them and grabs Paul by the throat, its breathing very loud*

**Paul** (*choking*) Quick, Soper! Your gun!

*Lord Soper rushes across to grab his rifle: he fires at the Mummy. The Mummy drops the unconscious Paul and makes for Lord Soper. Lord Soper fires again, then drops the rifle. The Mummy takes hold of him and flings him down* R. *Lord Soper crashes against the proscenium arch and collapses, unconscious. The Mummy turns, sees Niven lurking up* R, *grabs hold of the sarcophagus and rushes it at him. Niven dodges. The Mummy goes for him and grabs him*

**Niven** Oh no, old chap—careful . . .!

*The Mummy begins to choke him*

**Nancy** No! Not Daddy! Not Daddy!

*The Mummy drops the unconscious Niven, turns, sees her, holds out its arms. Music*

My lord . . . !

*It lumbers towards her, each crash of its huge feet marked musically*

My lord . . .

*She faints into its arms. The Mummy picks her up and moves down* C, *looking about it. The others begin to come round, choking. It turns and lumbers up towards the wall* C

**Paul** Stop him! Stop him!
**Lord Soper** How?

*With a tremendous crash, the Mummy walks through the upstage wall, a sound effect synchronised with his walk through the polystyrene blocks. Prior to this, slow-burning smoke-powder has been allowed to build up behind the wall, which now gives the effect of dust. A bright white lantern shines from outside into the Mummy through the dust and follows him as he lumbers up stage and off* L

**Paul** Quick! After him!

*Paul and Niven rush out after the Mummy*
*Lord Soper grabs up his rifle and turns to the audience*
**Lord Soper** Get yourselves a drink! This may take some time!
*Lord Soper rushes off after the others, as*

*the* CURTAIN *falls*

# ACT II

## Scene 1

*Ashayet's Palace. Night*

*The Pharaoh-God is in its position, with, beyond, a night sky on the cyclorama. Below, the Egyptian painted wall panels are set* R *and* L, *leaving open the centre, with the rear walls in position. Set* C, *just below the trap, is Ashayet's altar, covered with a black velvet cloth on which are visible strange designs*

*As the* CURTAIN *rises, a loud gong is heard. The lighting is dim, eerie, greenish. After a moment, the black-robed figure of Ashayet rises up behind the altar, on the trap, arms extended towards the Pharaoh-God. She turns front*

**Ashayet** Hail to Osiris, Lord of Eternity, King of Gods! Hail to Amun-Ra, perfect each day! Hail to Thoth, Lord of Dreams! Hail to Busiris, and to thee, Great Hathor, whose servant I be! Give me the power to waken my beloved! I need thy power! Give me the power! . . .

*The music behind this reaches a climax and then stops. She seems to falter and sway*

Ah! Ah . . .!

*She slowly sinks down behind the altar, shrinking in on herself, curling her hands in to her face, the music descending. Once she is out of sight, the music changes to a strange eerie piping—a suggestion of extreme old age. She crawls out from behind the altar to down* L, *her face concealed in the folds of her hood, one arm extended. It is withered, old, grey, ugly. She calls out in a thin, old, piping voice*

Kemal! Kemal . . .!

*Kemal hurries on* R

**Kemal** What is it? Have you found the right spell? (*Seeing her and recoiling*) Allah be merciful!

*She moans*

Forgive me. I've never seen you like this before.
**Ashayet** Do you think I advertise it, you fool? Call Anubis. I need more youth.
**Kemal** The river? You're going to bathe in the river?

**Ashayet** And show you the secret so that I lose my power over you? No, Kemal—the river is only necessary the first time. After that, the blood of a virgin suffices. I take it we have one in stock?
**Kemal** Yes, that little girl we abducted in Port Said.
**Ashayet** (*cackling*) Oh yes. Quite a rarity there.
**Kemal** Anubis says she's very weak. If he bleeds her much more, she'll die.
**Ashayet** What does that matter? She'll be dead in a few decades, anyway. I need her blood! Now!
**Kemal** (*calling off* R) Mr Rouse! Mr Rouse!

*Rouse runs on* R

**Rouse** Mr Kemal, sir?
**Kemal** Tell Anubis she needs more blood.
**Rouse** Oh that Mr Anubis, sir, he doesn't half give me the willies.
**Kemal** Do not worry. He will not harm you. Now hurry!

*Rouse hurries off* R

**Ashayet** (*using the hand of the "arm" to stroke her hidden hair*) I have to look my best for him, you see. He's not seen me for three and a half thousand years. It's important to make the right impression.
**Kemal** Yes . . .
**Ashayet** I sense a note of disapproval in your voice, Kemal.
**Kemal** I didn't expect so much death.
**Ashayet** Death? (*Laughing*) It's such a little thing. You hardly notice it once its happened . . . !
**Kemal** If the reward wasn't worth it . . .
**Ashayet** Yes, Eternal Life. But when one has loved as I have loved—a love that spans the centuries—a love so violent that it is the only thing that keeps me *sane* . . . !

*Rouse comes in* R *with a goblet*

**Rouse** Here's her blood, sir.

*Kemal goes to him quickly and takes it from him*

Tell her to go easy on it, sir. It's the last. I'm afraid the young lady isn't with us any more.
**Ashayet** Bring it to me! Quickly!

*Kemal hurries to her and hands her the goblet. She rises, facing up stage, drinking greedily. The music rises to a climax. As she finishes, she faces front, the black robe falling from her, young and beautiful again*

Ah! That's better.
**Kemal** My lady! (*He kneels before her*)
**Ashayet** That's good, Kemal. (*She puts the robe and the goblet on the altar*) Always remember your place is at my feet. (*She sings*)

## SONG 6. Maturity

When you reach my kind of age
Which is rare
Then you've reached a kind of stage
When you're aware
That it's time to leave the cloister
As a pearl must leave the oyster
And adorn a precious jewel
Of a princess fair to wear.

Maturity!
My youth is a memory
My age makes a gem of me
A fruit is sour till it's ripe
And then it sweetens into
Maturity!
It's made an adult of me
So worship the cult of me
Though older men are more my type.

**Kemal**  There's a moment later on
In one's career
When the bloom of youth has gone
It's very clear
And it's time for graduation
From a mere infatuation
To a deeper understanding
With a someone near and dear.

**Both**  Maturity!
We simply improve, you see
And then we remove the key
That was locking fortune's door
**Kemal**  And then it opens into
**Both**  Maturity!
**Kemal**  You're beautiful still to me
Bring sensuous thrills to me
Please say that I'm your paramour.

**Ashayet**  You will always be my true
And trusted friend
But the innocence in you
Will surely end
And though I love you like a brother
There will always be another
On whose form and grace and beauty
All my time I'll tend to spend.

     Maturity!
     It brightens the fires in me
     Those frightening desires in me
     For older wine is always best
**Kemal** It has the vintage of
**Both**  Maturity!
     Whatever will be will be
     From here to eternity
     Let's live our lives and damn the rest.

*At the end of the song, Kemal breaks* R *as Ashayet crosses exultantly to* DL

**Ashayet** And now—the Spell of Awakening! I am filled with power! (*Turning to the Pharaoh-God*) Oh thou that lieth dead but ever dreameth, hear, thy servant calleth! Hear me, O Mighty Hathor!

*She gestures. A gong sounds in the music and a puff of green smoke comes from behind the altar*

  In the tomb they have sealed him! But thou, O Mighty One, shall break his accursed bonds and set him free! The Dark Ones know thy name! I make the signs, I speak the words of power! Let him come forth, I say! Turn the key! Let him walk the earth once more!

*There is the huge sound of a crashing wall. Large blocks of stone are hurled across the upstage entrance from* L *to* R. *The heavy breathing of the Mummy is heard*

**Kemal** (*recoiling down* R, *staring off up* L) Allah be merciful!

*The Mummy appears in the gap, carrying Nancy*

**Ashayet** It worked! The spell worked!

*The Mummy moves forward to the altar*

**Kemal** But why has he brought Miss Niven here?

*The Mummy begins to lay Nancy down on the altar as Ashayet turns front and speaks savagely*

**Ashayet** Yes! Well, once before she came between us, and once again the gods have sent her to me for punishment!

*She draws her knife, crosses quickly up to Nancy and raises it to strike. The Mummy grasps her wrist. She cries out in pain and recoils to Kemal*

*The Mummy picks up the goblet from the altar and lumbers off down* L. *The magnified sound of his heavy breathing and the thud of his feet continues to be heard as he goes*

  What in the name of Ra is he looking for?
**Kemal** It's unbelievable! He's alive! Just as you said he would be!
**Ashayet** Only in one sense. He has lain in the dark for three and a half aeons. His mind has gone, for the moment. He remembers only the simplest things. But this is good—it means he can be controlled.

Act II, Scene 1                                                                 57

*During the above, the Mummy returns with the goblet and goes to the altar, bending over Nancy*

**Kemal** He's found what he wanted.

*The Mummy dips fingers in the goblet and flicks them at Nancy's face. Treble notes on the piano*

**Ashayet** Water.

*The Mummy repeats the action, then steps back as Nancy dizzily sits up, his free hand held out, almost touching her face*

**Nancy** Kemal! Ashayet! What are you doing here? What am *I* doing here?

*She turns, sees the Mummy, screams, and faints again. The Mummy begins to pat her face gently—gently, for him, but great lumbering blows as far as Nancy is concerned, rocking her head, magnified*

**Kemal** Stop him! He'll kill her!

*Ashayet restrains the Mummy. Nancy sits up, jumps off the table and runs to Kemal*

**Nancy** Kemal!

*The Mummy puts down the goblet and starts around the altar to pursue Nancy. Ashayet runs quickly forward and presses him back*

**Ashayet** No, beloved, no! Forget the girl! She is nothing! It is I, your Ashayet, you should be thinking of! It is I who found you! I who brought you back! The important thing now is to restore your youth! You are too old, Inmutef. Look at you. The girl—she wouldn't have you, looking like this. You must bathe again. And drink the blood—(*turning and bestowing an evil smile on Nancy*)—of a virgin.

**Kemal** No!

**Ashayet** (*running to him and hissing*) Be quiet, you fool! It is the only way! Let him keep her until the ceremony is over, and then it will be too late!

**Kemal** No. For too long now have I done your evil bidding, old woman!

**Ashayet** (*recoiling, furious, hands to face*) You think to insult me?

**Kemal** You'll not have this girl, Ashayet. The answer is no. This is the end.

**Ashayet** You think so? (*Going behind the altar and pointing at him*) Look at him, Inmutef! He has the girl! He steals her from you! He harms her! He is your enemy! Kill, Inmutef! Kill! Kill him!

*The Mummy advances on Kemal, his breathing sounding louder*

**Kemal** No! No! Stop him, you fool!

*Kemal releases Nancy, who cowers down* R. *Ashayet laughs madly as Kemal draws his knife and plunges it into the Mummy's chest, but the Mummy simply removes it and drops it on the altar. He advances on Kemal, who backs behind the altar, Ashayet dancing up* L, *drawing her knife and threatening his rear. The Mummy takes his throat by one hand and lifts him. Bring up the trap at this point and Kemal will seem to have been lifted up in the air by the Mummy. Theatres without this facility, should attempt some sort of lifting device, since the effect is too good to lose. The Mummy tosses Kemal aside and he falls L of the altar. The Mummy then turns and advances on Nancy. Ashayet enjoys Kemal's death a moment, and then goes to the Mummy*

**Ashayet** That's it, my beloved—that's it!

*The Mummy picks up Nancy*

And now to the river. Let us bathe together, as we did before, all those years ago.
**Paul** (*off*) There's a light over this way!
**Nancy** (*screaming*) Paul!
**Ashayet** Quickly, Inmutef—quickly! (*She leads the way behind the altar*)
**Paul** (*off*) Over here! I think I heard her!
**Nancy** Paul!
**Ashayet** In here! It conceals the old way! Quickly!

*She presses a button on the altar and they drop down smoothly out of sight. For theatres without traps, sliding panels can be built into the set, or even the suggested design panels used*

*Niven, Paul and Lord Soper rush in*

**Niven** Incredible! A fully preserved Egyptian Temple! From the outside, it just looks like a fully unpreserved subsidized theatre.
**Lord Soper** Never mind your poor attempts at wit, Niven. Look over here.
**Niven** Good Lord, it's Kemal!

*Niven and Paul hurry to Kemal and kneel over him*

**Lord Soper** Is he all right?
**Paul** He's dead, you fool.
**Niven** Not quite. His throat's crushed.

*Kemal makes a gargling sound in his throat, trying to point to the trap*

What is it, old chap?

*Kemal gargles. Lord Soper gargles in reply, inquiringly*

*Kemal dies*

He's gone, I'm afraid, poor devil.
**Lord Soper** Don't waste your sympathy on him, Niven. He tried to kill us back there.
**Paul** (*wandering* C *behind the altar, fiddling with it*) He seemed to be trying to tell us something.
**Niven** I wonder who killed him.
**Lord Soper** The Mummy, of course. No ordinary mortal's got that kind of strength.
**Paul** He was pointing over here somewhere.

Act II, Scene 1

*Paul inadvertantly touches the button and vanishes, with a yell*

**Niven** What was that?
**Lord Soper** I haven't the faintest idea. (*Moving quickly* R, *rifle at the ready*) Where's Conway got to?
**Niven** He was right behind us.
**Lord Soper** Well, he's not there now. (*Rounding on him*) Are you two up to something?
**Niven** I assure you I'm as puzzled as you are.
**Lord Soper** (*prowling off* R) Conway? Conway? Stop fooling, man, this is serious.
**Niven** (*going behind the altar*) He seemed to be over here somewhere.

*Niven accidently touches button and vanishes, with a yell*

**Lord Soper** (*rushing back on*) Was that you, Niven? (*Looking around*) Now you're at it, are you? Well, you won't get the better of me! Nobody gets the better of me! (*To Kemal*) You'd have found that out, had you lived long enough.

*He notices that Kemal's rigid arm is still pointing*

Hallo! He's pointing somewhere! (*He hurries to him, kneels and sights along the arm. He rises and proceeds cautiously behind the altar*) Careful, Rodney. (*Looking around*) There's nothing here at all.

*Lord Soper leans the butt of his rifle casually on the button and vanishes, with a yell*

*The Lights fade to a Black-out. During it, there is the sound of hammering, and Lord Soper's voice is heard*

(*Off*) I'll get you for this, Kemal! No, I won't—somebody's already got you. But I'll get *somebody*—just you wait and see . . . !

### Scene 2

*Below the Palace*

*Music. After a moment, it fades to broken minor chords and Paul's voice is heard*

**Paul** (*off*) Hallo? Anybody about?

*He comes on* R *on the elevated area*

Can't see a thing in this damned gloom.

*He strikes a match and a small pool of light collects on the elevated area*

Hallo? (*He nearly walks right off the edge*) Ah! (*Peering over*) That was a close shave . . . (*Looking* L) Hallo! (*Moving* L *on the elevated area and peering at the ground*) Footprints! Three people, by the look of it. (*Determinedly*) Best foot forward, Conway old chap. No old mummy's going to steal *my* girl.

*Paul creeps off* L

(*Off*) Hallo? Hallo?
**Niven** (*off*) Hallo? Hallo?

*Niven comes on* R *on the elevated area*

Conway? Nancy? Anybody there? Hallo? (*Looking* L) Hallo! (*Moving* L *on the elevated area and peering at the ground*) Footprints! Four people, by the look of it. (*Creeping off* L) Hallo? Hallo?

*Niven goes off* L. *Lord Soper springs on* R *on the elevated area, rifle at the ready*

**Lord Soper** What was that? I thought I heard something. (*Crossing slowly* L) Do you know what I think, Rodney? I think somebody's trying to pull the wool over your eyes, that's what I think. (*Turning back suddenly, rifle at the ready*) Always remember what mummy said—cover your rear. (*Turning back and peering at the ground*) Hallo! Footprints! Looks like the entire cast of *Chu Chin Chow* passed this way. (*Creeping off* L) Hallo? Hallo?

*Lord Soper exits* L

*The music continues. The two central wall panels slide apart to* R *and* L, *revealing a diagonal ladder set below the upper level. A dim light builds on the stage below*

*Ashayet comes on up* L, *followed by the Mummy carrying Nancy*

**Nancy** At least tell me where you're taking me to!
**Ashayet** You'll find out soon enough. (*Calling softly off* R) Anubis! —Anubis!

*Music. With a bound, Anubis leaps on up* R. *He wears the full dog-mask, stripped to the waist and carries a sword*

*Nancy screams*

Don't worry, my dear—he's with me. A pleasant fellow, but a little . . (*Tapping her head*) He thinks he's a god.
**Nancy** He's not the only one around here.

*Anubis waves his arms and mumbles to Ashayet*

**Ashayet** Good. (*To the Mummy*) The water is building, my beloved. And when the moon is right, the power will come to it.

*Anubis mumbles*

Don't worry—I have a virgin in mind.
**Nancy** What do you mean?
**Ashayet** Nothing, my dear. Just relax. You're quite safe.
**Paul** (*off, shouting*) Nancy? Was that you?
**Nancy** (*screaming*) Paul! Over here! (*She squirms free from the Mummy's grasp and drops to her feet*)

## Act II, Scene 2

**Ashayet** Anubis! Silence her!

*Anubis crosses to Nancy and puts hand over her mouth*

It is them—your enemies! They have found the way in! Destroy them!

*The Mummy hesitates, hands reaching out for Nancy*

Do as you are told! Kill, Inmutef! Kill! Obey me!

*The Mummy turns and lumbers off up R*

As for you, my dear—won't you come this way?

*Ashayet goes to the R wall panel and touches a switch. It slides open and Anubis drags the struggling Nancy in*

That's it, my dear. Straight ahead.

*The panel closes behind Ashayet, Anubis and Nancy. Paul runs on L, above*

**Paul** Nancy? Nancy? Where are you? Nancy . . . (*He pauses in his pacing and taps the floor of the elevated area*) Hallo! That sounded hollow. (*He kneels and examines the floor*) Careful. It could be a trap. (*He opens it*) It *is* a trap . . . Ah well, nothing ventured, nothing gained. (*He climbs carefully down the ladder, closing the trap behind him*) This place is like a blasted maze. (*Skirting the open trap in the stage, he begins examining the wall panel L. It suddenly shoots open and he recoils with a yell*) Ah!

*But it is only Niven who steps out, the panel closing behind him*

**Niven** It's all right, Conway, it's only me. Odd sort of a place. Whenever you touch anything, a wall opens. And what's this here? (*Indicating the stage trap*) Looks like an old well. (*Kneeling and burying his face in it, his voice echoing with reverberated microphone assistance*) Well, well, well, it *is* an old well. Fightfully deep, as well. (*Scrambling to his feet*) Which way do you suggest we go?
**Paul** Only one way left—down here.
**Niven** Very well, my boy—lead on.

*As they begin to go off up L, the heavy breathing and measured footsteps of the Mummy is heard*

**Paul** Look out! It's the Mummy!
**Niven** Coming this way!

*They scrabble at the wall panel up L, then peer around the stage. Paul indicates the ladder*

**Paul** Quick! Up the ladder!

*They rush to it and climb up, colliding with one another, crashing against the roof*

It won't open!
**Niven** What do we do?
**Paul** (*indicating the stage trap*) Down here!

**Niven** But it's hundreds of feet deep!
**Paul** We'll just have to hang on!

*Gritting their teeth, they lower themselves into the "well", just the tips of their fingers showing*

*The Mummy lumbers on up* L, *looking about suspiciously. It crosses* R, *almost stepping on their fingers*

*Paul's and Niven's heads raise up, teeth gritted, and drop down again as the Mummy crosses back* L

*The Mummy goes off* L

*Paul's and Niven's heads reappear*

It's all right. It's gone.

*Paul pulls himself out: but as he comes up, Niven's pained face goes slowly down*

**Niven** Conway! I can't hold on any longer! I'm going!

*Paul flings himself flat as Niven's hands fly up and down, half Paul's body going down into the "well" as he "catches" Niven. He finally heaves him out*

Oh, thank you, Conway. You saved my life. Where's the brute got to now?

**Paul** (*moving up* L *and peering off*) He's lurking at the end of the corridor. I'm afraid we're stuck here.

**Niven** Oh well—we're safe enough for the moment.

*The sudden sound of a heavy footstep is heard above*

What's that?

**Paul** Ssh! (*He indicates above as the footsteps continue*)

*A prowling Lord Soper appears, looking suspiciously about him*

*Paul puts finger to lips and climbs slowly up the ladder. He hits his head on the floor and Lord Soper reacts backwards violently, aiming his rifle at it. Pause. Lord Soper puts down his rifle and bends to put an ear to the floor at the same time as Paul is putting an ear to his ceiling*

Hallo?

*Lord Soper grabs his rifle and leaps to his feet*

**Lord Soper** Conway? Where the devil are you, man?
**Paul** In a lower chamber. But the trap only opens from your side.
**Lord Soper** Ah! (*Seeing the trap and opening it*) Ah!
**Paul** (*coming up half-way through the trap, relieved*) Oh thank heavens, Soper. We'd given you up for lost.
**Lord Soper** Yes, I'm sure you had. (*Peering down past him at Niven*) And Niven too. Quite a cosy little twosome, aren't we?
**Niven** (*peering up the ladder*) I don't know what you mean.

Act II, Scene 2 63

**Lord Soper** Don't play with me, Niven. I get very jumpy when people play with me. Me trigger finger goes quite spasmodic.
**Paul** What's he talking about?
**Niven** I haven't the faintest idea.
**Lord Soper** Won't wash, old lad. You see, I've worked out your little plan.
**Niven** What little plan?
**Lord Soper** You were going to get there first, weren't you? You were going to find the River of Life and keep it all to yourselves, weren't you?
**Paul** Of course we weren't.
**Lord Soper** Of course you were!
**Paul** Of course we weren't! Dash it all, there ought to be enough immortality for everybody, don't you know.
**Niven** If it exists at all.
**Lord Soper** (*aiming his rifle through trap at him, with bared teeth*) Don't say that, Niven! Don't—ever—say—that.
**Niven** Look here, Soper, you've been under a bit of a strain—the heat—the journey—being engaged to Nancy—it's only natural.
**Lord Soper** I'm perfectly calm, Niven!
**Niven** Yes, I can see that, but why don't you just leave everything to us, eh?
**Lord Soper** Oh, so that's your game, is it?
**Niven** What game?
**Lord Soper** Going to have me certified, are you? Going to have me put away, like my first wife tried? (*During this, he indicates with jerks of his rifle that Paul should descend the ladder and join Niven*)
**Niven** Of course not. We wouldn't do a think like that.
**Paul** Well, *I* would.
**Niven** Quiet, Conway.
**Paul** Well, look at him—he's going off his chump.
**Lord Soper** (*ominously calm, beginning to descend the ladder*) Do you know, Conway—I rather think you mean that.
**Paul** I do.
**Lord Soper** Yes, but it's a pity really. Puts me in a rather difficult position, don't you think? (*He slips off the ladder, hangs on by the skin of his teeth, reaches up to close the trap*)
**Niven** No!
**Paul** The trap!

*Lord Soper closes the trap with a laugh and drops to his feet below the ladder*

**Lord Soper** Don't worry, chaps—nobody's getting out of here—(*searching above his head, pressing a spring and jumping forward as the two central wall panels close behind him*)—nobody at all.
**Paul** Well, I suggest *you* do, Soper. They can do wonders with heads these days. And there must be *some* good in you, otherwise Nancy would never have fallen for you.
**Lord Soper** (*circling below them to* L, *jerking with rifle, indicating they should move* R) You're right, Conway—she *did* fall for me. And she'd

fall for me again with you two out of the way. (*Bringing the rifle up to his shoulder*) I rather think I'm going to arrange a little accident.
**Niven** You'll never get away with it!
**Lord Soper** I got away with it with my first wife.
**Paul** You blighter!
**Lord Soper** Quite correct. Now then—who's first?
**Niven** (*pushing in front of Paul*) I've had my life, Conway.
**Paul** (*pushing in front of Niven*) No, Professor, I insist.
**Lord Soper** Stop arguing! We'll take it as it comes! (*Taking aim*) You first, Conway.

*To the sound of heavy breathing, the Mummy appears behind Lord Soper*

**Paul** Look out, Soper! Behind you!
**Lord Soper** Oh really, Conway.
**Niven** There's a mummy right behind you!
**Lord Soper** You must think I'm a child, falling for an old trick like that. And now . . .

*Lord Soper crouches a little forward in taking his final aiming position, and the Mummy's hands crash together with a great booming sound, missing his head by a fraction. He turns, sees it, screams in fear, drops the rifle, staggers back, and falls into the well, hanging on for dear life*

Conway! Niven! Help!

*The Mummy begins to advance on him. Niven steps forward to help him, but Paul restrains him*

**Paul** Don't be a fool, Professor!
**Niven** Well, we can't just leave him there to die! Divert the thing! Divert it!
**Paul** How?
**Niven** How the hell should *I* know? Just do it!

*Paul dances to the other side of the Mummy and pulls faces at it*

**Paul** Yah! Ugly old Mummy! Can't catch me!

*The Mummy turns on him, swinging an arm, and Paul ducks. During the following, Niven helps Lord Soper out of the trap*

My dad's a policeman, my dad's a policeman! (*He ducks under the Mummy's swinging arms, runs to the ladder, climbs half up it, pulls faces*) Mnyah! Mnyah!

*The Mummy goes for Paul and he jumps down, dodging past it down* L

**Niven** It's all right, Conway—you can stop him chasing you now.

*Paul turns to look at Niven and the Mummy gets him by the throat, strangling him*

I said you can stop him chasing you now!
**Paul** (*in a strangled voice*) Don't tell *me*! Tell *him*!

## Act II, Scene 2

**Niven** Oh well, it's all my fault really, I suppose—and it's time I saw Nancy's dear mother again.

*He kicks the Mummy up the backside. It releases Paul and turns on him. Niven cocks his fists*

**** I'll hold him off! You two run for it!
**Paul** Never!
**Lord Soper** Yes! Yes! Good idea! (*Trying to rise and falling*) Ah! I've hurt my ankle!

*The Mummy grabs Niven by the throat. Paul looks around desperately for a weapon, and—suddenly hit by an idea—pulls a tin whistle from his pocket and plays it. Captivated by the music, the Mummy releases Niven and turns on him. Paul moves slowly around and above the well. The Mummy follows him, and steps in*

*For a moment the Mummy teeters on the edge of the well, then it falls*

*There is a long descending whistle and a distant echoing thud. All peer down the well, panting, relieved*

**Paul** Oh well, that's the end of him.
**Niven** Are you all right, Soper, old chap?
**Lord Soper** Yes, thanks. I don't know what to say, Niven. You saved my life.
**Niven** Yes, I suppose I did, really.
**Lord Soper** And Conway too. You're white men—both of you—absolute white men!
**Niven** Think nothing of it. We knew you'd come round in the end. After all, when you've been on as many of these expeditions as I have, you get to know the signs. The heat and the fever get to a chap, and—well—he's just not himself for a while.
**Lord Soper** I must say, you're taking this awfully well.
**Niven** Not at all, old chap. Not at all. After all, you're British.

*A follow spot hits Lord Soper, and he stiffens*

Come to think of it, we all are.
**Paul** Quite.

*Paul conducts the Band into the introduction to the song. Lord Soper indicates pleased surprise—"for me?"—then sings*

### SONG 7: **British Heroes**

**Lord Soper** When all on your own in the desert
Under a merciless sun
Nothing but sand in your canteen
No ammo left in your gun
A band of hostile tribesmen surround you
And bury you there still alive
Who comes along and digs you out when they've gone?
Why, Carruthers of the M-I-Five.

| | |
|---|---|
| **All** | Carruthers of the M.I.Five |
| | British heroes know how to behave<br>Always calm in the face of sheer hell<br>British heroes are fearless and brave<br>With impeccable timing as well. |
| **Niven** | When hacking your way through a jungle<br>In blistering tropical heat<br>You step on a trap in the bushes<br>And hang from a tree by your feet<br>Cut down by a horde of wild natives<br>Who prepare you for their cooking pot<br>Who swings in on a vine, gets you out just in time<br>Jungle Jim and his intrepid lot |
| **All** | Jungle Jim and his intrepid lot |
| | British heroes know how to behave<br>With a dashing but delicate touch<br>British heroes don't panic or rave<br>And never perspire very much |
| **Paul** | When freezing to death in the Arctic<br>And visibly nearing your end<br>Body all ravaged with frostbite<br>Polar bears eating your friend<br>You pray to the Lord to have mercy<br>Please make death quick when it comes<br>But then who swoops in low and makes a perfect three-point touch-down in the snow?<br>Why, it's Biggles and his trio of chums |
| **All** | Biggles and his trio of chums |
| | British heroes know how to behave<br>They're the tops and they're second to none<br>British heroes come through a close shave<br>And do it again just for fun |
| | So if you're up against it somewhere<br>On land, sea or air<br>And the odds are unfair<br>Then don't ever despair<br>'Cos British heroes<br>I say British heroes<br>Will always be there |
| (*Spoken*) Oh. Yes. | |

*They congratulate one another, shake hands, pat one another on the back*

**Lord Soper** (*to Niven*) I say, would you mind passing me my rifle?
**Niven** Not at all, old chap.

Act II, Scene 2

**Lord Soper** (*shaking Paul's hand*) Conway, I am repentence itself.
**Paul** Not at all, old boy.
**Niven** (*handing him the rifle*) Here you are, Soper.
**Lord Soper** (*taking it and moving* R) Thank you so much.
**Paul** (*to Niven*) I must say, I was absolutely wrong about him. He's not such a bad stick, after all.
**Niven** I knew it all the time, dear boy.
**Lord Soper** Now then . . .!

*Minor chords*

(*Turning and aiming the rifle at them*) Where were we?

*Paul and Niven clap their heads, and throw their hats on the ground*

**Paul** You absolute rotter, Soper!
**Lord Soper** Yes! I'm sorry, chaps, but I *am* going to find the River of Life first and I *am* going to keep it all to myself. (*Aiming carefully*) And this time, there'll be no interruption.
**Niven** I'm not so sure about that. You see, there's a cobra right behind you.
**Lord Soper** (*turning quickly*) What? What? Aaagh! . . .

*Lord Soper drops the rifle, steps back quickly and falls down the well. There is a long despairing yell, then a distant echoing thud*

**Niven** Poor old Soper. Shame, really.
**Paul** (*going to pick up the rifle*) Good thinking on your part, though, Professor. Since the Mummy was real the time before, he believed in your imaginary cobra.
**Niven** Yes—except it wasn't imaginary.

*There is a loud hiss and a head strikes at Paul. He retreats with a yell*

I'm glad, though. Makes me feel less like a murderer somehow.
**Paul** Well, he had it coming to him. Come on, Professor, we must find Nancy!

*Paul decides he would not know how to use the rifle and drops it into the well*

*Paul and Niven hurry off* L

*Minor music, as the scene changes*

### Scene 3

*A Small Chamber*

*The trap closes, and the two central wall panels draw aside to reveal the body of a slave-girl, hanging from chains. Behind her, the gauzed Egyptian panels form a background*

*Ashayet comes in* R *and crosses* L, *followed by Anubis, who drags Nancy* RC

**Nancy** Where are you taking me to? Let me go! (*She sees the dead girl and screams*)
**Ashayet** (*to Anubis, angrily*) What is this dead virgin still doing here? If I've told you once, I've told you a hundred times—don't clutter the place up with virgins once they've been drained! Call Rouse!
**Anubis** Rouse! Rouse!

*Rouse runs in* R

**Ashayet** What is this dead virgin still doing here?
**Rouse** (*hurrying up to the girl*) I'm sorry, miss—I didn't know what you did with your empties.

*Rouse carries the dead girl out* R

**Nancy** What happened to her?
**Ashayet** She provided blood—just as *you* are about to, my dear.
**Nancy** I don't think Inmutef will let you. He rather likes me.
**Ashayet** He will do as he is told when the time comes—once it is a choice between you and his youth. (*To Anubis*) Get her ready.

*Anubis chains Nancy in the girl's place*

**Nancy** You're very sure of yourself, aren't you?
**Ashayet** I ought to be. I'm a lot older than you.

*Rouse enters* R

Curse that Mummy! What's he up to? It shouldn't take him this long to kill a few people. (*To Rouse*) Where is Inmutef?
**Rouse** I didn't even know he was up and about, miss.
**Ashayet** I'd better go and look for him. You come with me. (*To Anubis*) You stay and guard her. And be careful. She is a clever woman, and you are a rather stupid man. Come, Rouse.

*Ashayet exits* R, *followed by Rouse*

**Nancy** (*after a pause*) Well—here we are, then. (*Pause*) I'm sorry, I didn't quite catch your name.

*Anubis goes to her and indicates his name on the chain around his neck*

Anubis. Oh yes, one of those old gods. I've heard Daddy talk about you. Lord of the Dead, aren't you? Invented embalming? Very clever. I'm not very creative in that way, I'm afraid. (*She stretches languidly*) Isn't it hot?

*Anubis cocks his jackal's head, looking at her body*

I'd do anything to get out of this dress. It's really clinging to me. But then, if I did, you'd have to take these chains off, and that nice lady wouldn't like that, would she?

*Anubis thinks about this and shakes his head*

I *do* like her, you know. She reminds me of Mary Pickford. Very similar

# Act II, Scene 3

voice. Of course, I've never *heard* Mary Pickford's voice, but I'm sure they're frightfully the same. (*Pause*) You're very handsome, you know.

*Anubis cannot believe she said it*

Such lovely ears and such a long, pointed nose. I like a man who's interestingly different. (*She carefully arranges a pose and sings*)

### SONG 8: **Get Down**

I betcha think ya look cute
From your toes to your snoot
You're a real rooty-tooty, mine host
I ain't complaining
But you're gonna need training
To do just what Momma loves most
If you wanna thing with me
You've got to let it all hang free
Just loosen up and I'll show you how
But if Momma starts to frown
And Momma says, "Get down"
Momma means get down right now

I bet you think you're a hound
When you're out and around
Bet you come on like a wolf with the chicks
Well, that number's over
I've seen through you, rover
'Cos I ain't no kid from the sticks
If you wanna score with me
You've got to show a slight degree
Of virtuosity, and then—wow!
But if Momma starts to frown
And Momma says, "Get down"
Momma means get down right now

I'm gonna seize you, squeeze you
Tease you, please you
Don't cha know we're two of a kind?
I'm gonna take you, shake you
Make you, break you
And then I'm gonna blow your mind

So come on, fill my cup
You impetuous pup
Light me up and set me in flames
Make with the growlin'
The hootin' and the howlin'
And teach me some cute doggy games
If you wanna swing with me
You've got to get down on your knee

I've just got to see you grovel and bow
But if Momma starts to frown
And Momma says, "Get down"
Momma means get down right now

But when Momma says, "Get down"
Momma means get down—
You know she means get down
You got to get down
Right now!

*At the end of the song she sings an extended finish, coaxing Anubis nearer and nearer. Finally she kicks him in the groin. He howls dismally. She uses her leg to lift the keys from his belt, releases herself, goes and hands the keys back to him*

Thanks. I hope it didn't hurt too much. (*She turns to leave,* R)

*Loud breathing is heard: Paul enters* R, *dressed as the Mummy*

*Nancy backs away*

Oh no! And I nearly made it!

*The Mummy turns on Anubis and indicates he should leave. Anubis protests. The Mummy makes an even more imperious gesture*

*The miserable Anubis leaves, tail between his legs*

*The Mummy advances on Nancy, who backs away further*

Now keep away. I'm warning you. I can kick in very nasty places.

*She kicks him in the groin and runs past him towards the exit* R. *The Mummy doubles up and Paul's muffled voice is heard*

**Paul** Heavens to Betsy!

*Nancy skids to a halt, and turns*

**Nancy** What did you say?
**Paul** Thank God for all these bandages, that's all I can say.
**Nancy** Paul, is that you?
**Paul** Well, who do you think it is? Do I *look* like a rotten old mummy?
**Nancy** Well—yes. What are you playing at?
**Paul** Your father and I found a nestful of old mummies and we thought it would be a good idea if I disguised myself—fool everybody, so to speak.
**Nancy** Well, you certainly fooled *me*.
**Ashayet** (*off*) Inmutef is *here*? You say he's *here*?
**Paul** Quick! She's coming back! Disguise yourself! (*He holds out his arms*)
**Nancy** What as?
**Paul** A kidnapped girl, of course!
**Nancy** Oh—right.

*She jumps into his arms, causing him to stagger and meander in a circle*

*Ashayet enters R, followed by Anubis and Rouse*

**Ashayet** My beloved, you've come back to me! Now at last we can begin. To the River of Life! Lead on, my darling!

*Paul walks into the proscenium arch L*

**Nancy** (*hissing*) What are you doing?
**Paul** (*hissing back*) I can't see a thing through these bloody bandages.
**Ashayet** (*going to Paul and leading him R*) My beloved, where do you go? This way—deeper into the earth—much deeper.

*Paul carries Nancy off R*

We must hurry, Anubis. He is growing visibly weaker. (*To Rouse*) You know what you have to do?
**Rouse** No, miss.
**Ashayet** (*to Anubis*) You know what you have to do?

*Anubis grunts, nods*

Then do it!

*There is a loud crash off, and a yell from Paul*

Not that way, beloved! Don't you even remember where the River of Life is?

*Ashayet hurries off after them*

*Rouse turns, to find Anubis's face close to him, and yells in fear*

*Anubis curses and waves his sword, then lopes off after Ashayet*

*Rouse moves down C. The Lights check down and the panels close*

**Rouse** Honestly, Nobby, lad, you haven't half let yourself in for it this time. I know they say join the Navy to see the world, but this is ridiculous. Dead virgins, people drinking blood, mummies walking all over the place, and that nutcase with that dog's head . . .

*There is a howl off from Anubis. Rouse jumps out of his skin*

Mind you, that Professor and his daughter, Nancy—now they're a nice pair. Except they're not paying the bill, and Mr Kemal's always come across with the readies. Well, Nobby, lad, you'll have to decide soon.

*Rouse looks about him and goes off L*

*The central wall panels open*

### Scene 4

*The Base of the Well*

*The sprawled bodies of the Mummy and Lord Soper are revealed, Soper practically sitting on the Mummy, one of its huge arms over his chest. He groans, wakes up, and sees his predicament. With great care, he lifts off the hand, rises, peers around—but he is trapped, there is no way out. There is sudden heavy breathing. The Mummy lifts its head. Lord Soper laughs nervously, edging as far away from it as possible as it rises*

**Lord Soper** Erm—thanks for breaking my fall, old chap. You, of course, can't be killed—I should have thought of that.

*The Mummy lunges at him and Lord Soper ducks to* R

Look here, Mr Inmutef, this wasn't *my* idea! They chucked me down as well, you know! I was on *your* side—really I was!

*The Mummy lunges and Lord Soper ducks past him* L

It was those swine up there—particularly that Conway fellow. He's an absolute cad.

*The Mummy gets him by the throat and forces him down*

Do you know, he's engaged to your girl-friend!

*The Mummy releases him. Choking, Lord Soper continues*

Actually *engaged* to her—there's infidelity for you.

*The Mummy breaks* R

If I were you, I'd punish him (*To himself*) Good idea, Rodney! Good idea! (*He rises, goes to the Mummy, puts an arm round his shoulders*) In fact, tell you what, I'll help you—point him out to you.

*The Mummy turns and Lord Soper hastily dodges away*

I knew you'd see it my way. Obviously a fellow of class.

*The Mummy lumbers* L, *feeling off behind the wall* L. *Lord Soper dodges* R

You'll never break through there, old son—not even you. It's feet of solid rock.

*The Mummy pushes. There is a mighty sound of crashing rock, and dust blows into the area*

Oh well, can't be right all the time—not even a Tory Peer. (*He picks up his rifle and peers off cautiously after the Mummy*) Better let him get well ahead, Rodders—don't entirely trust the brute.

*Lord Soper slips out after the Mummy*

*Loud, sombre music is heard, and the Lights fade to a Black-out*

### SCENE 5

*The River of Life*

*The Lights reveal the River of Life, a God carved out of the solid rock, set above the trap, from one of whose eyes a trickle of water runs down its body and into the trap. The sound of running water, gentle eerie music is heard*

## Act II, Scene 5

*Ashayet comes on,* R, *to* LC, *followed by Paul carrying Nancy to* RC, *and Anubis to* R

**Ashayet** Here we are, my beloved—at last!
**Nancy** What is this horrid little grotto, anyway?
**Ashayet** Horrid little grotto! This, you poor fool, is the ancient River of Life!
**Nancy** What, that little trickle?
**Ashayet** Yes—a mere trickle now—but when the moon is in the position of power and shines through the vent in the roof above, you will see the water turn to a coloured mist—and whoever bathes in the mist is immortal.
**Nancy** But where do *I* come in?
**Ashayet** Isn't it plain, my dear? Immortal life does not mean immortal youth. For that, the water must be sprinkled with the blood of a virgin, and the bather enter regularly.
**Nancy** You're mad.
**Ashayet** On no, it's quite simple. A small incision—here. (*Taking Nancy's wrist*) The vein remains open, and the blood drips into the river below until the body is drained. (*Breaking down* L) Ah, how many beautiful young girls has it taken to keep me as I am over the centuries! And now my darling needs it too! It will make him young and beautiful again.
**Nancy** (*to Paul*) Just imagine! Even more young and beautiful than you are now—a girl could go mad.
**Ashayet** Enough! This is no time for levity! Let Anubis strap her in the place!

*Anubis takes Nancy from Paul and drags her up to the river. He begins to chain her in place, then climbs the ladder to lock her manacles from above. Paul weaves about, not sure what to do. Ashayet leads him down* L

Yes, yes, I know, my darling—you care for her still—but she need not die—we can release her before then. In fact, if you wish, she may also bathe, and everything will be all right . . .
**Nancy** What are you planning—some kind of ghastly ancient Egyptian ménàge a trois?
**Ashayet** (*moving up to her, softly*) No, my dear, much more subtle than that. He will be distracted during the change, and by the time he recovers . . . (*Shrugging*) A tragic accident. He won't even blame me.
**Nancy** I wouldn't bet on it, you awful old witch!
**Ashayet** Anubis! The key!

*Anubis drops the key to her as she turns to Paul*

Come, my beloved, let us go and prepare. No harm will attend her, I promise. Come.

*Ashayet goes off* R

*Paul lumbers after her, running back to Nancy once Ashayet has gone*

**Paul** (*hissing*) I'll get the key and be back as soon as I can. Try not to panic.

*Paul lumbers off* R

**Nancy** Panic, indeed!

*Anubis drops to the base of the ladder and growls at her as he follows Ashayet off* R

The only people panicking around here are the poor dears trying to rescue me.

*Loud breathing is heard as Niven, dressed as the Mummy, enters* L

(*In panic*) Oh my God, it's the real one! He's back! Help! Help!

*The Mummy puts its hands on its hips and glares at her*

**Niven** Oh for heaven's sake, Nancy, stop making that awful din. Don't you recognize your own father when you see him?
**Nancy** Daddy, is that you?
**Niven** Of course it is. If we waited for Conway to rescue you, we'd *all* need a dip in the River of Life. Must say I'm frightfully glad to see you. We were getting a bit worried. How do those chains work?
**Nancy** There's a key. Paul's gone off to get it.
**Niven** Which way did he go?
**Nancy** Down there.
**Niven** Oh jolly good, I'll toddle off after him, then.

*Paul enters holding the key*

**Paul** It's all right, Nancy, I got the key . . . Oh my God, the *real* Mummy—it's still alive!

*Paul rushes off* R

**Niven** Conway! Conway!

*Niven runs off after Paul*

**Nancy** This is ridiculous. The place is full of mummies. Oh, for an ordinary, normal, smiling, friendly face . . .

*Scowling in concentration, rifle at the ready, Lord Soper comes on* L

Rodney!
**Lord Soper** Oh, there you are. What are you doing up there?
**Nancy** I'm being sacrificed or something. Turn me loose before that crazy woman comes back.
**Lord Soper** Ashayet! She's here?
**Nancy** Yes, she—

*Niven rushes on* R, *sees Lord Soper, yells and runs off* R. *Paul rushes on* L, *sees Lord Soper, yells and rushes off* L

—went that way.

Act II, Scene 5                                                                 75

**Lord Soper** (*trying to fathom out what he has just seen*) That way? You say she went that way?
**Nancy** Yes.
**Lord Soper** Well, I'd better get after her then. (*He prowls* R)
**Nancy** Yes, but Rodney—Rodney—aren't you going to release me first?
**Lord Soper** No, I don't think so. Want to find out how this River of Life works first. Might need you for that.
**Nancy** But she's going to kill me!
**Lord Soper** Yes, sorry about that. (*He goes* R)
**Nancy** Oh Lord . . .!

*With a sound of heavy breathing, the Mummy lumbers on* L

Oh thank heavens, Daddy, there you are! Did you get the key off Paul all right? You're breathing rather hard, you know. You must be out of condition.

*The Mummy moves slowly towards her*

Daddy? Paul?

*The Mummy claps its hands together with a mighty booming sound*

Oh my God, it's the real one! Help! Help!

*The Mummy advances on Nancy*

*Ashayet runs on* R

**Ashayet** No, look, there's no time for that now—the moon!—the mist is forming!

*Mist begins to spill out of the trap*

Quickly, Inmutef, your prayer to Thoth!

*A shaft of light shines from high up down* R. *The Mummy lumbers down* R *hands held out to the "moon", kneels and begins making obeisance*

Anubis!

*Anubis comes on* R

The vein!

*Anubis advances on Nancy, sword drawn*

**Nancy** No! No!

*Anubis cuts Nancy's wrist. The water turns red: the mist turns pink. Ashayet waves her hands in the mist, laughing madly. Anubis backs up* L. *Nancy screams*

**Ashayet** Perfect. In a few minutes, my dear, it will all be over. He will be mine, and you will be dead.

*Rouse runs on* L

**Rouse** Oh no you don't! The worm has turned! I'll help you, miss!

*With a bound, Anubis appears in front of Rouse. With a yell, Rouse backs off. Anubis slashes with his sword, Rouse ducks. Anubis runs him through the shoulder and he rolls down* L

**Ashayet** A minor interruption, my dear. And now . . .

*Paul runs on* L, *his Mummy's head off*

**Paul** Oh no you don't! I'll rescue you, Nancy—mummy or no mummy!

*Anubis leaps behind Paul, puts the sword over his head and strangles him, throwing him down close to Rouse*

**Ashayet** Quickly, Inmutef—quickly—the moon is passing! Time to bathe, my darling—time to bathe!

*The Mummy rises and lumbers towards the mist*

**Nancy** (*lifting her head weakly*) Inmutef—you loved me once. You swore it would last through all eternity. Well, is *this* what you want? Is it?

*The Mummy hesitates*

**Ashayet** Pay no attention, Inmutef! Everything will be all right, I promise! Step in, Inmutef! (*Angrily, with great authority as he still hesitates*) Step *in!*

*The Mummy prepares to climb in. Ashayet crosses to Nancy, hissing in triumph*

As for you, my dear—goodbye.
**Nancy** No!

*As the Mummy is about to climb in, the Pharaoh-God suddenly glows with an unearthly light and a deep, booming voice comes out of it*

**Niven's Voice** (*disguised*) Inmutef! High Priest of Amun-Ra! Listen to me! I command thee! Mighty Hathor speaks to thee!

*Ashayet, the Mummy, Anubis, all face up to the God, and drop to their knees,* R, C *and* L

The Gods are angry, Inmutef. You must stop this. Restrain the old woman. She is twisted with jealousy and hate. Release the girl, Inmutef, before it is too late. Release her. I command thee. All the Gods command thee.

*The Mummy rises to his feet and makes towards Nancy*

**Ashayet** Anubis! Stop him!

*Anubis goes to the Mummy, but it beats its mighty hands either side of Anubis's head, and he dies* LC. *The Mummy breaks Nancy's shackles and lowers her to the ground,* RC. *It tears a piece of bandage off itself and binds her wrist*

**Niven's Voice** You have done well, Inmutef! The Gods are pleased. And now . . .

## Act II, Scene 5

*Lord Soper appears* R

**Lord Soper** And now enough of this nonsense! Come out from behind that statue, Niven! Come out, I say!

*A shamefaced Niven, Mummy's head off, megaphone in hand, appears on the top level, from behind the Pharaoh-God*

You see, Inmutef? It's as I told you! They are your enemies! Well, leave *this* one to me! (*He aims his rifle*)
**Nancy** No, Inmutef! Stop him! For *me*, Inmutef! Stop him!

*The Mummy takes the rifle from Lord Soper and slowly bends it in two*

**Lord Soper** Oh no! My new Remington!

*The Mummy grabs Lord Soper*

No! We're friends, remember?

*The Mummy breaks his back over his knee and throws him up* R, *then turns on Ashayet. She backs slowly away from him and around* C

**Ashayet** No—no, my beloved—I did it for you—I did it for us—I . . .

*Ashayet falls into the mist with a scream. The Mummy clutches at its face as if splashed by the water and staggers to its knees. There is a loud hissing, bubbling, screaming. The ageing, disintegrating figure of Ashayet (dummy) rises up out of the mist and falls back in. The mist fades away. Rouse, Paul and Niven peer down into it*

**Niven** What on earth happened?
**Rouse** She just seemed to age and crumble away, like.

*Paul hurries to Nancy as Niven climbs down the ladder*

**Paul** Nancy, darling, are you all right?
**Nancy** Yes, I think so.

*The Mummy suddenly lifts itself to its knees, hands held out to her. Music.*

**Niven** Be careful!

*They back off a little, but the Mummy merely holds the hands out imploringly to Nancy. Soft music. The Mummy collapses*

**Nancy** Poor Inmutef. He really did love me, you know.
**Paul** Yes. (*Pause*) Funny sort of River of Life, though. I thought if it was sprinkled with the blood of a virgin . . .
**Nancy** Ah.

*They stare at her*

Well. You see. There *was* something I'd been meaning to tell you, Paul. I don't know quite how to put this, dear, but you remember Roger Fulbright . . .
**Paul** (*in agony*) Not Roger Fulbright!

**Nancy** Well, yes. It was his home-made wine, really. Nobody would drink it except me. And—well—I rather think it spoiled Ashayet's plan...

**Paul** Oh Nancy—(*he moves down* R)—

*Sad music*

—how could you?

**Niven** (*stepping between them and joining their hands together*) There, there, my boy, don't be too harsh on her. After all, this *is* nineteen twenty-two, and she hasn't had the benefit of her mother's touch for some time—come to think of it, neither have I—and it *did* save our lives—even if it has ruined the only River of Life in existence. (*He turns to the River of Life unhappily*)

**Rouse** Never mind, sir. There'll be other places, other times, other adventures...

*Niven perks up*

**Niven** Quite right, my boy—quite right.

*They sing*

SONG 9: Sailing Away (reprise)

**All** (*except Kemal, Ashayet, Soper, Inmutef*)
>The siren is a-blowin'
>The adrenalin is flowin'
>We're sailin' away
>Sailin' away
>Off to sandy places
>In search of an oasis to stay

*The dead people come to life, Ashayet rising up out of the trap*

>The siren is a-blowin'
>The adrenalin is flowin'
>We're sailin' away
>Sailin' away
>Off to sandy places
>In search of an oasis to stay
>The wake behind us bubbles
>Like smoke our cares and troubles
>Are trailin' away
>Trailin' away
>Cruisin' down the delta
>You can swelter as you're sailin' away.

**The Rest**
>Remember I'll be with you
>Though you may be so far away
>Goodbye dear friends, I'll miss you
>Till you come home some day.

| | |
|---|---|
| **All** | If life has no mystery<br>Then what is life at all?<br>Oh yeah . . . |

                            CURTAIN

# FURNITURE AND PROPERTY LIST

```
                              cyclorama
wwwwwwwwwwww                                           wwwwwwwwwww
black travellers
                         escape stairs
                                    ruined wall
                                    sliding panels
              pillar        window                        pillar
                            profile pillars + header
           rostrum area                    trap
           exchangeable sliding panels    God position

pillar              pillar                  pillar         pillar
                                cloth position

              trucked piano         trap
              position


profile pillar                                        profile pillar
```

NOTES:
Certain properties can be set during the action of the scene prior to that in which they are required: these are indicated in the following list.

Exchangeable sliding panels consist of:

4 double-sided panels, all representing rough stone walls on one side: when reversed 2 of them show Egyptian wall paintings and the other 2 show shelves of books.

2 single-sided gauzed panels, representing Egyptian sliding doors.

## ACT I
### SCENE 1

| | |
|---|---|
| *On stage:* | Pharaoh-God |
| | Piano |
| | Black travellers closed |
| | Rear sliding wall panels closed |
| | Egyptian wall paintings at A and D on downstage track |
| | Gauzed Egyptian sliding doors at B and C on upstage track |
| *Off stage:* | Bandages and Mummy change (**Inmutef**) |
| *Personal:* | **Ashayet**: knife |
| | **Mahu**: knife |
| | **Amenhotep**: knife |

# The Mummy's Tomb 81

### Scene 2

| | |
|---|---|
| *Strike:* | God |
| *Set:* | Desk and chair (by **Niven**). *On desk:* roll of papyrus, breakable clay tablet, dagger, dressing |
| | Museum exhibit |
| | Black travellers open |
| | Window in position |
| *Slide:* | Gauzed Egyptian doors from B and C to offstage on upstage track |
| | Bookshelf panels from offstage to B and C on upstage track |
| *Off stage:* | Breakable vase (**Farouk**) |
| | Chloroform cloth (**Farouk**) |
| *Personal:* | Nancy: handbag with compact |
| | Niven: magnifying glass |
| *During scene:* | Set carpet, standard lamp, picture on rear wall, chair: all in position behind bookshelf panels at B and C |

### Scene 3

| | |
|---|---|
| *Strike:* | Desk |
| | Chair |
| | Museum exhibit |
| *Slide:* | Bookshelf panels from B and C to A and D on upstage track |
| | Egyptian wall panels from A and D to offstage on downstage track |
| *Off stage:* | Tea trolley. *On it:* trick omelette pan, flambé stove, cutlery, blancmange (**Mrs McGuinness**) |
| | Hat, coat, scarf (**Niven**) |
| | Telephone on tray (**Mrs McGuinness**) |
| | Telephone handset (**Farouk**) |
| *During scene:* | Exchange Egyptian wall panels for rough wall panels off stage on downstage track: packing cases behind bookshelf panel at A |

### Scene 4

| | |
|---|---|
| *Strike:* | Window |
| *Set:* | Black travellers closed |
| *Slide:* | Wall panels from off stage to B and C on downstage track |
| | Bookshelf panels from A and D to off stage on upstage track |
| *Personal:* | **Niven:** torch |
| | **Paul:** torch |
| | **Soper:** pistol, wallet with notes |
| | **Kemal:** cigarette in holder |
| *During scene:* | Open rear wall panels: strike carpet, chair, standard lamp, picture: set chair with **Nancy** tied in it. |
| | Clear packing cases: exchange bookshelf panels for wall panels off stage on upstage track |

## Scene 5

| | |
|---|---|
| *Strike:* | Pillars, header |
| *Set:* | Trap closed |
| | Bollard, rope (by **Rouse**) |
| | Ladder (by **Harry**) |
| | Black travellers open |
| *Slide:* | Wall panels from off stage to B and C on upstage track |
| *Off stage:* | General luggage |
| | Rifle (**Soper**) |
| | Bandoliers (**Soper**) |
| | Pistol at belt (**Soper**) |
| | Spare rifle in case (**Soper**) |
| | Back pack (**Soper**) |
| | Carrier bag (**Paul**) |
| | Binoculars, mapcase (**Niven**) |
| *Personal:* | **Mrs McGuinness**: handbag with handkerchief |

## Scene 6

| | |
|---|---|
| *Strike:* | Bollard and rope |
| *Set:* | Pillars, header |
| *Off stage:* | Oilskins, sou'westers (**general**) |
| | Ship's wheel (**Kemal**) |
| | Telescope (**Kemal**) |
| | Mugs on tray (**Paul**) |
| | Ship's railing (**Stage Management**) |
| *During scene:* | Preset bead curtains fixed behind A and D: open rear wall panels |

## Scene 7

| | |
|---|---|
| *Set:* | Palm tree (by **Servant**) |
| | Cane chair (by **Servant**) |
| *Slide* | All wall panels off stage |
| *Off stage:* | Roll of carpet (**Paul**) |
| | Eastern-looking string instrument (**Paul**) |
| | Camera on tripod (**Niven**) |
| | Fly whisk (**Soper**) |
| | Towel (**Nancy**) |
| | Silver tray with iced tea in glasses (**Servant**) |
| *Personal:* | **Servant**: coins |

## Scene 8

| | |
|---|---|
| *Set:* | Dhow |
| | Cloth of fleecy clouds |
| *Off stage:* | Rolled-up tent (**Rouse**) |
| | Folded chair (**Rouse**) |
| | Back pack (**Rouse**) |
| *During scene:* | Strike bead curtains: preset Egyptian wall panels to A and D on downstage track: open rear wall panels: set ruined wall up stage |

# The Mummy's Tomb

## Scene 9

| | |
|---|---|
| *Strike:* | Cloth |
| *Slide:* | Ruined wall down stage behind profile pillar |
| *Off stage:* | Special stage lamp for silhouette |
| | Tent (**Cast**) |
| | Folding stools (**Cast**) |
| | Picnic hamper with plates, glasses, apples, champagne, etc. (**Cast**) |
| | Cactus in pot (**Nancy**) |
| | Blankets (**Niven**) |
| | Rifle (**Taureg**) |
| | Camel's head (**Stage Management**) |
| | Trick cobra for silhouette (**Stage Management**) |
| | Prop cobra (**Kemal**) |
| | Piano (**Rouse**) |
| *Personal:* | **Kemal**: knife |

## Scene 10

| | |
|---|---|
| *Strike:* | Tent up stage of cloth |
| *Set:* | Cloth |
| *Slide:* | Downstage ruined wall off stage |
| *Off stage:* | Water bottle (**Niven**) |
| | Back pack (**Paul**) |
| | Pack with spade (**Rouse**) |
| *During scene:* | Complete striking tent: strike upstage ruined wall: exchange Egyptian wall panels at A and D with rough wall panels at A and D on downstage track: build breakable wall at B and C: set god in position: set up slow-burning smoke powder to create dust effect when wall breaks: close black travellers: strike special silhouette lamp: stand by with hand-held lamp special, to follow **Mummy** through smoke after wall breaking |

## Scene 11

| | |
|---|---|
| *Set:* | Sarcophagus with **Mummy** inside |
| | Trap closed |

## ACT II

### Scene 1

| | |
|---|---|
| *Set:* | Black travellers open |
| | God in position |
| | Rear wall panels closed |
| | Egyptian wall panels at A and D on downstage track |
| | Rough wall panels preset behind them at A and D on upstage track |
| | Trap open |
| | Altar downstage of trap and masking it |
| | False arm under altar (for **Ashayet**) |

| | |
|---|---|
| *Off stage:* | Goblet of blood (**Rouse**) |
| | 2 pieces of broken wall bricks (**Stage Management**) |
| *Personal:* | Kemal: trick knife |
| | Ashayet: knife |

SCENE 2

| | |
|---|---|
| *Strike:* | Altar |
| | God |
| *Set:* | Black travellers closed |
| *Slide:* | Wall panels from A and D to B and C on upstage track |
| *Off stage:* | Cobra head (**Stage Management**) |
| *Personal:* | Paul: matches, tin whistle |
| | Anubis: sword |
| *During scene:* | Set diagonal ladder behind B and C up to trap in top level of rostrum |
| | Strike ladder after use: set gauzed Egyptian door panels in front of rear walls: set trick chains to allow movement during Nancy's song: set dead virgin hanging in chains |

SCENE 3

| | |
|---|---|
| *Set:* | Trap closed |
| *Slide:* | Wall panels to A and D on upstage track (behind Egyptian wall panels) |
| *Personal:* | Anubis: key |
| *During scene:* | Strike gauzed panels and chains: set rifle |

SCENE 4

| | |
|---|---|
| *Slide:* | Wall panels at B and C to A and D on upstage track (behind Egyptian wall panels) |
| *Off stage:* | Smoke powder (**Stage Management**) |

SCENE 5

| | |
|---|---|
| *Set:* | God |
| | River of Life |
| | Ladder (same position as in dockside scene) |
| | Trap open |
| *Slide:* | Egyptian wall panels A and D to offstage on downstage track (leaving rough wall panels at A and D on upstage track) |
| *Off stage:* | Dry ice machine in trap (**Stage Management**) |
| | Megaphone (**Niven**) |
| | Dummy of Ashayet in trap (**Stage Management**) |
| | Bendable rifle (**Soper**) |
| *Personal:* | Anubis: key |

# LIGHTING PLOT

Special effects required: cloud projectors (numbers depending upon size of cyclorama and cloth)—slow, fleecy clouds on downstage cloth, fast storm clouds on upstage cyclorama
Property fittings required: practical standard lamp

ACT I SCENE 1

*To open:* Dim moody lighting picks out the set. As the CURTAIN rises a spot picks out Paul at the piano.

| | | |
|---|---|---|
| Cue 1 | Paul: "... Eternal, Life!"<br>*Build acting area together with specials underneath rostrum* | (Page 1) |
| Cue 2 | Exeunt of **Inmutef** and **Guards**<br>*Lose specials underneath rostrum* | (Page 3) |
| Cue 3 | Amenhotep: "Behold your lover's punishment."<br>*Check down main stage, build specials underneath rostrum to see through gauze* | (Page 3) |
| Cue 4 | Ashayet: "Inmutef! Inmutef...!"<br>*Restore previous lighting* | (Page 3) |
| Cue 5 | Paul: "... secrecy is *guaranteed*..."<br>*Build specials underneath rostrum* | (Page 3) |
| Cue 6 | Amenhotep exits<br>*Lose specials underneath rostrum, check down all stage level areas* | (Page 4) |
| Cue 7 | Paul: "... fades into oblivion."<br>*Fade to Black-out except for spot on* **Paul** | (Page 4) |

ACT I SCENE 2

| | | |
|---|---|---|
| Cue 8 | Paul: "... at the British Museum..."<br>*Build state. Lose spot on Paul. Bright daylight cyclorama. Window backlit to indicate light source* | (Page 4) |
| Cue 9 | Beginning of the Song<br>*Check down, more colourful state. Pink spots on singers* | (Page 9) |
| Cue 10 | End of song<br>*Restore previous lighting* | (Page 10) |
| Cue 11 | **Paul** and **Soper** exit<br>*Check down acting area* | (Page 11) |

ACT I SCENE 3

| | | |
|---|---|---|
| Cue 12 | Nancy and Farouk exit<br>*Crossfade to warm, central area, artificial light, specials underneath rostrum, practical standard lamp, dark blue night cyclorama* | (Page 12) |

| | | |
|---|---|---|
| *Cue* 13 | **Niven:** "Niven here." *Spot picks out* **Farouk** *on top level* | (Page 13) |
| *Cue* 14 | **Farouk** exits *Fade spot* | (Page 13) |
| *Cue* 15 | **Mrs McGuinness** exits to below rostrum *Fade to Black-out* | (Page 14) |

ACT I SCENE 4

| | | |
|---|---|---|
| *Cue* 16 | **Niven, Paul** and **Soper** exit *Small dim area central and specials underneath rostrum* | (Page 15) |
| *Cue* 17 | **Farouk** opens trap *Add special in trap* | (Page 15) |
| *Cue* 18 | **Paul:** " . . . somebody certainly did." *Even out acting area* | (Page 16) |

ACT I SCENE 5

| | | |
|---|---|---|
| *Cue* 19 | **Nancy:** (*off*) "Oh shut up, Rodney!" *Crossfade to bright cold morning effect on cyclorama and top level, a little below* | (Page 19) |
| *Cue* 20 | End of song *Build cold light to include stage level* | (Page 20) |

ACT I SCENE 6

| | | |
|---|---|---|
| *Cue* 21 | **Harry:** "It's coming on to rain!" *Crossfade to very dim blue area down* C | (Page 24) |
| *Cue* 22 | **Kemal:** "It's easing off, I think!" *Small build on state* | (Page 25) |

ACT I SCENE 7

| | | |
|---|---|---|
| *Cue* 23 | **Rouse:** "Good old Cairo!" *Crossfade bright warm full up, all areas* | (Page 26) |
| *Cue* 24 | **Nancy** leaves top level *Check down top level* | (Page 28) |
| *Cue* 25 | **Ashayet** enters *Check down main acting area a little. Pink opera spot on* **Ashayet.** *Fade once she is in position* | (Page 29) |

ACT I SCENE 8

| | | |
|---|---|---|
| *Cue* 26 | **Kemal** exits *Crossfade to moonlight on downstage cloth and downstage stage area, picking out dhow sails, together with fleecy clouds, travelling from* L *to* R | (Page 30) |
| *Cue* 27 | **Ashayet:** "All the gods live." *Build cold special on* **Ashayet** *from* L | (Page 31) |
| *Cue* 28 | End of song *Fade special* | (Page 32) |

The Mummy's Tomb 87

| | | |
|---|---|---|
| *Cue* 29 | Dhow goes in action<br>*Adjust lighting, downstage linear area only* | (Page 34) |

ACT I SCENE 9

| | | |
|---|---|---|
| *Cue* 30 | **Rouse:** "I'm going to be her slave."<br>*Crossfade dim amber light, all areas, including cyclorama, together with fast storm clouds moving from* L *to* R | (Page 36) |
| *Cue* 31 | **Ashayet:** "You will see."<br>*Fade out clouds. Dilute amber. Effect of coming desert sunset* | (Page 36) |
| *Cue* 32 | As tent is constructed in song<br>*Fade upstage areas* | (Page 38) |
| *Cue* 33 | **Taureg** exits<br>*Begin slow check down to night* | (Page 41) |
| *Cue* 34 | As **Kemal** crosses down L<br>*Snap on silhouette special* | (Page 42) |
| *Cue* 35 | As they half move towards tent<br>*Snap off silhouette special* | (Page 43) |
| *Cue* 36 | **Soper, Kemal, Paul** exit<br>*Fade to Black-out* | (Page 43) |

ACT I SCENE 10

| | | |
|---|---|---|
| *Cue* 37 | As soon as cloth is in position<br>*Build very bright hot full up on cloth and downstage areas* | (Page 44) |

ACT I SCENE 11

| | | |
|---|---|---|
| *Cue* 38 | **Kemal** exits down trap<br>*Fade to Black-out* | (Page 47) |
| *Cue* 39 | Grating of stone opening<br>*Build low angle white special along floor from apparent low entrance down* L. *Follow on with slow dim state inside tomb* | (Page 47) |
| *Cue* 40 | **Mummy** is revealed<br>*Adjust state* | (Page 47) |
| *Cue* 41 | Grating of stone closing<br>*Fade out low special, follow on with slow check down to very dim state* | (Page 50) |
| *Cue* 42 | **Mummy** breaks through wall<br>*Follow* **Mummy** *from upstage through smoke with hand-held special* | (Page 51) |

ACT II

ACT II SCENE 1

| | | |
|---|---|---|
| *Cue* 43 | CURTAIN rises<br>*Dim eerie lighting, top and bottom levels, together with specials underneath rostrum* | (Page 53) |

| | | |
|---|---|---|
| Cue 44 | Ashayet rises up out of the trap<br>*Add spot on* Ashayet | (Page 53) |
| Cue 45 | Ashayet sinks out of sight behind altar<br>*Fade out spot* | (Page 53) |
| Cue 46 | Ashayet drinks blood, becomes young<br>*Build brighter state* | (Page 54) |
| Cue 47 | Soper vanishes behind altar<br>*Fade to Black-out* | (Page 59) |

ACT II SCENE 2

| | | |
|---|---|---|
| Cue 48 | Paul lights match<br>*Build small state, top level only* | (Page 59) |
| Cue 49 | Soper exits<br>*Add dim state to stage level, together with specials underneath rostrum* | (Page 60) |
| Cue 50 | As wall panels close<br>*Fade area on top off level and specials underneath rostrum* | (Page 61) |
| Cue 51 | Niven: "After all, you're British."<br>*Snap spot on* Soper | (Page 65) |
| Cue 52 | Song<br>*Use spots* | (Page 65) |
| Cue 53 | End of song<br>*Fade limes* | (Page 66) |

ACT II SCENE 3

| | | |
|---|---|---|
| Cue 54 | Paul and Niven exit<br>*Crossfade to dim acting area downstage, warm area up C warm specials underneath rostrum* | (Page 67) |
| Cue 55 | Nancy sings<br>*Add spot* | (Page 69) |
| Cue 56 | End of song<br>*Fade lime* | (Page 70) |
| Cue 57 | Panels close behind Rouse<br>*Lose warm area up C and specials underneath rostrum* | (Page 71) |

ACT II SCENE 4

| | | |
|---|---|---|
| Cue 58 | Rouse exits<br>*Crossfade to specials underneath rostrum only* | (Page 71) |
| Cue 59 | Soper exits<br>*Fade to Black-out* | (Page 72) |

ACT II SCENE 5

| | | |
|---|---|---|
| Cue 60 | When set<br>*Build dim but colourful eerie light top and bottom levels for River of Life, together with special in trap* | (Page 72) |

| | | |
|---|---|---|
| *Cue* 61 | **Nancy** strapped to her place<br>*Bring up spot on* **Nancy** | (Page 73) |
| *Cue* 62 | **Ashayet:** ". . . your prayer to Thoth!"<br>*Add moon special* R | (Page 75) |
| *Cue* 63 | As **Nancy's** wrist is cut<br>*Add red special to water* | (Page 75) |
| *Cue* 64 | As **Inmutef** is about to climb in trap<br>*Check down all areas, build eerie special on the god* | (Page 76) |
| *Cue* 65 | **Mummy** releases **Nancy**<br>*Fade spot and red special* | (Page 76) |
| *Cue* 66 | **Soper:** "Come out, I say."<br>*Restore previous lighting* | (Page 77) |
| *Cue* 67 | As dummy of **Ashayet** goes down<br>*Fade moon special and trap special* | (Page 77) |
| *Cue* 68 | **Niven:** "—quite right."<br>*Bright full up on top and bottom areas* | (Page 78) |

# EFFECTS PLOT

*N.B.* This plot assumes that live microphones are available for actors to do all heavy breathing for the Mummy, hissing for snakes, etc. This is much the best and most effective way of providing and timing the sounds. In fact, in the original production, a great many of the sounds were produced "live" in this way: Mummy's footsteps, Beating Hands, Falling Whistles, Distant Thuds, etc.

Two tape decks are required for the following plot, since some of the effects mix into others

## ACT I

### Scene 1

*No cues*

### Scene 2

*No cues*

### Scene 3

| | | |
|---|---|---|
| *Cue 1* | **Niven:** "... at any minute." *Telephone bell rings* | (Page 12) |

### Scene 4

| | | |
|---|---|---|
| *Cue 2* | With scene change *Lapping water, foghorns* | (Page 14) |
| *Cue 3* | **Niven:** "And pray God we're in time." *Fade out lapping water, foghorns* | (Page 15) |
| *Cue 4* | **Farouk:** "... Yes, I have!" *Clock strikes twelve* | (Page 15) |
| *Cue 5* | **Farouk** opens trap *Lapping water only, louder* | (Page 15) |
| *Cue 6* | **Farouk's** dying fall, pause *Splash, and fade out lapping water* | (Page 15) |

### Scene 5

| | | |
|---|---|---|
| *Cue 7* | **Nancy:** (*off*) "Oh shut up, Rodney!" *Seagulls, ships' hooters* | (Page 19) |
| *Cue 8* | As **Rouse** begins to sing *Fade out seagulls* | (Page 19) |
| *Cue 9* | End of song *Seagulls, continuing* | (Page 20) |

# The Mummy's Tomb

| | | |
|---|---|---|
| Cue 10 | **Soper:** "I wouldn't like to say."<br>*Loud ship's hooter* | (Page 22) |
| Cue 11 | As **Mrs McGuinness** begins to sing<br>*Fade out seagulls* | (Page 23) |

### Scene 6

| | | |
|---|---|---|
| Cue 12 | **Harry:** ". . . it's coming on to rain."<br>*Loud wind, thunder, waves* | (Page 24) |
| Cue 13 | **Kemal:** "It's easing off, I think!"<br>*Check above down a little* | (Page 25) |
| Cue 14 | **Rouse:** "Good old Cairo!"<br>*Fade out wind, thunder, waves* | (Page 26) |

### Scene 7

*No cues*

### Scene 8

| | | |
|---|---|---|
| Cue 15 | As dhow comes on<br>*Gentle rippling water* | (Page 30) |
| Cue 16 | As **Ashayet** begins to sing<br>*Fade out rippling water* | (Page 31) |
| Cue 17 | **Soper:** "It was standing still."<br>*Faint sound of white water* | (Page 33) |
| Cue 18 | **Kemal:** "It's a cataract!"<br>*Crash up volume on white water* | (Page 33) |
| Cue 19 | **Soper:** "Get me into the bank!"<br>*Crash of dhow hitting rock* | (Page 33) |
| Cue 20 | As dhow goes<br>*Fade down level of white water* | (Page 34) |
| Cue 21 | **Nancy:** "There she goes now."<br>*Fade out white water* | (Page 34) |

### Scene 9

| | | |
|---|---|---|
| Cue 22 | **Rouse:** "I'm going to be her slave."<br>*Loud wind, continuing* | (Page 36) |
| Cue 23 | **Ashayet:** "You will see."<br>*Fade wind out* | (Page 36) |

### Scene 10

*No cues*

### Scene 11

| | | |
|---|---|---|
| Cue 24 | **Ashayet:** "Leave it to me."<br>*Grating of moving stone, opening* | (Page 47) |
| Cue 25 | **Ashayet:** (*off*) "Release the stone!"<br>*Grating of moving stone, closing* | (Page 50) |
| Cue 26 | **Mummy** walks through wall<br>*Very loud crash of falling wall* | (Page 51) |

## ACT II

### Scene 1

| | | |
|---|---|---|
| Cue 27 | **Ashayet:** "... walk the earth once more!" *Loud crash of falling wall* | (Page 56) |

### Scene 2

No cues

### Scene 3

No cues

### Scene 4

| | | |
|---|---|---|
| Cue 28 | **Soper:** "It's feet of solid rock." *Loud crash of falling wall* | (Page 72) |

### Scene 5

| | | |
|---|---|---|
| Cue 29 | As Lights come up on scene *Gentle, rippling water* | (Page 72) |
| Cue 30 | **Nancy:** "Help! Help!" *Fade out water* | (Page 75) |
| Cue 31 | **Ashayet** falls into the trap *Loud hissing, bubbling, screaming, continuing for a while, fading as dummy sinks out of sight* | (Page 77) |

## SPECIAL EFFECTS

The play calls for the following:
 1 practical pistol (can then double all further rifle shots)
 1 omelette pan, wired for flambé pyro effect (optional)
 1 camera on tripod, wired for pyro flash (optional)
 1 flashbox behind altar for Act II, Scene 1.
 1 slow-burning smoke effect to create dust of crashing wall (essential)
 1 dry-ice machine for River of Life (essential)

MADE AND PRINTED IN GREAT BRITAIN BY
LATIMER TREND & COMPANY LTD PLYMOUTH
MADE IN ENGLAND

www.ingramcontent.com/pod-product-compliance
Ingram Content Group UK Ltd.
Pitfield, Milton Keynes, MK11 3LW, UK
UKHW021842140426
5217IPUK00022B/1550